Manu

Manu

Recipes and Stories
from My Brazil

Manoella Buffara

En route to Cerro Azul to see one of my producers, Divonei and Nerli Mariano, the owners of Vale e Cia.

Entrance of Fazenda Ferrador, where the lamb served at Manu is raised.

Foreword by
Dominique Crenn

The Atlantic Forest in Mandirituba is home to many species of stingless bees.

Sisterhood, Sharing, and Giving Back

Since I first met Manu over a decade ago, I have had a special connection with her. Something resonates from that incredible woman that is difficult to articulate. It's an energy and a light that comes from somewhere deep inside her, and it's what I and so many connect with. Giving back to others is at the core of Manu's beliefs. Her relationships with her friends and family, restaurant, and community are first and foremost in her life. I know that she will be the first one to give no matter what I ask.

Manu and I are similar in many ways. We have thrived in this male-dominated industry whose roots, no matter how hard we try to scrub them clean, are still tarnished with ideas of sexism, inequality, and harassment. To be a woman in this environment is not easy; to prosper here is almost impossible. Your body wears down after years of abuse in hot and unrelenting kitchens; your mind weakens from the stress and (more often than not) mental abuse. The only way to rise above the noise is to believe in yourself and your values and never waver. But this type of confidence you must witness to imitate.

Manu, like me, grew up in the kitchen of her grandmother. Seasons were spent surrounded by food and the love that can only be found in a kitchen and around a dining-room table. My grandmother devoted her life to the farm, working grueling hours while keeping a home and raising a family. I spent many formative years quietly watching her, admiring her strength and resilience, and knowing that I would only be so lucky to fabricate myself into such a beautiful person. Manu saw her grandmother through the same lens. She spent many summers and winters in her grandmother's kitchen, learning heirloom recipes and old-world techniques and gaining an appreciation for food that is often lost on younger generations. Our grandmothers built homes where food was the centerpiece for conversations, moments for learning, triumphs, laughter, and tears. I am grateful for these women and those all over the world who are pillars of strength and raising the next generation of greatness. An inherited maternal compass now guides Manu—she steers through life, making a point to care for everyone along the way. She doesn't live her life in search of awards or recognition; she knows that true wealth comes from the heart and from family and friends. She constantly gives to the underserved communities around her, creating urban gardens and education around sustainability and remaining close to the people and culture that cultivated her. Manu's impact on the earth may be small, but her contribution to her community is immeasurable.

Manu and I acknowledge that our place in this world is insignificant. We believe our real purpose in life is to give back to others, and sharing such a simple and clear intention has created a beautiful and honest sisterhood between us. My favorite memories with Manu include us doing what we love—breaking bread and sharing stories and laughs. I recently sat down to reflect on all our special moments together and sift through old photographs. Each one has a warm quality. Our smiles are so real that you can almost hear the laughter emanating from the photograph, if you listen closely. I found myself sitting in a quiet room, all alone, laughing out loud as I vividly recalled every amazing moment.

I believe that the greatest chefs in this world are not only chefs—they are true humans. They have a greater purpose. They are drawn to feeding people because that is the basis of love, culture, and humanity. Manu Buffara is a true human, the bridge to the next generation of strong, conscientious and thoughtful chefs, and she is one of the greatest in the world.

Foreword by
Alex Atala

An Ocean Wave (or "She's a Sensation")

One of the first times I went to Noma, I was informed that a Brazilian trainee was working at the restaurant. I remember being intrigued by how she got there. By that time, René Redzepi was already considered among chefs to be a virtuoso, a talent not to be missed. However, his name was still unfamiliar to those outside the restaurant industry. It was far from obvious that an aspiring Brazilian chef might seek the opportunity to learn cooking under his tutelage.

Later, I discovered she was Manu Buffara, a southerner from Curitiba. To be at Noma five years before it was recognized as the best restaurant in the world says a lot about Manu. While studying in Piedmont, she was impressed by an article about Redzepi in *Apicius*, a Spanish and English journal of haute cuisine. Without a second thought, she asked to spend some time there. When Manu and I became friends, she told me they said yes to her request, though they didn't understand why a Brazilian would want to spend the winter working in Copenhagen. That's Manu. She never plays it safe; she always wants to push herself and her abilities to be a better cook.

And what a great cook that trainee became!

Manu Buffara is amazing. She is one of the chefs I like most to exchange ideas with and talk about ingredients. We can also laugh about life or share a burger at In-N-Out. After dealing with the best ingredients, she understands that fast food sometimes can fit perfectly at the end of a fancy night. And if the following day is a weekday, she'll wake up to run or play tennis. But if it's a Sunday, she'll find her way to church to pray.

One of Manu's strengths is that she understands her environment so well. She started using native Brazilian honey long ago, and she fights for its popularization and commercialization. Manu knows where to find the best wild *Lactarius* mushrooms, which grow in southern Brazil, and all the ways to cook them (and she's skilled with other varieties as well). Manu is the one who told me Brazilian seawaters have geoduck clams. She is a tireless researcher and always curious about what to eat and how an ingredient can be added, cooked, or prepared for a dish. Like me, Manu likes to source her ingredients outdoors. She has a strong connection with the sea and everything that comes from it. She often gathers seaweed along the coast of Paraná and Santa Catarina, 125 miles (200 kilometers) from her restaurant Manu. I often compare her to water: she always finds her way, even in the harshest winds. Or better, in her case, she is like an ocean wave that drums with elegance, presence, and strength. She brings astonishment and joy to those who sit at her table.

It is impossible to talk about Manu without mentioning one of the most admired chefs in the modern kitchen. His name is Michel Bras. They both are far from the gastronomic axis of their countries. Bras lives and cooks in Auvergne, a region completely separate from the Paris-Lyon axis and rich with good ingredients and traditions. He has revolutionized French cuisine with his love for food and ingredients. I see a parallel reality and an analogous project at the restaurant Manu. Manu is also a mother, warrior, cook, chef, environmental fighter, and superwoman—in Curitiba, a city outside the Rio–São Paulo axis. If Manu was in one of these big cities, she would have greater international prestige. This is partly why I admire her so much. She shunned great gastronomic poles for a signature kitchen in Curitiba, with all its challenges. Like Michel Bras, she is in love with good ingredients. Her work with Brazilian local fishing communities, her relationship with her producers, and her commitment to her vegetable garden all move me. And she does it so coherently and affectionately.

Manu knows her job and runs the show in a kitchen. She understands flavor, texture, composition, and how to create an impressive menu. It isn't difficult to cook well, but it is hard to assemble a sequence of dishes that amazes everyone seated at the table. She gives simple and precise orders to whoever is working at her side. She likes to teach and discuss why to include (or exclude) this or that herb, salt, sugar, or vegetable in a recipe. She also cares about her team. When traveling to cook abroad, chefs tend to bring with them the best-trained team, to facilitate cooking in other conditions. Manu does not think this way. She always brings the team members who would best take advantage of the experience of cooking elsewhere, meaning that she herself has to work harder. And she's content with that. This amazes me and all the important chefs I know, and this is rare in the high-end gastronomy world. Aside from cooking well, she is easygoing, has a ready laugh, embraces her country roots, and is fond of learning.

In the first year of FRUTO, the food festival I've organized in São Paulo since 2018, Manu was part of the culinary team invited to cook for speakers during the pre-opening event. We were on a farm and had to improvise on the grill. We had a lot of incredible and fresh Brazilian ingredients available to create dishes, but before any of us could think about how we'd prepare the food, she was serving a pineapple with oyster sauce that we all remember to this day.

Manu's kitchen is subtle. Yet nothing in a dish by Manu Buffara is by chance. There is a reason for the carrot pickles to be there, for the cauliflower to be done that way, and for the shrimp (prawns) to be cooked or served raw. And she is not afraid to remove a sauce or herb if it does not work in a dish.

In addition to her prowess in the kitchen, she is a champion for her environment. She fights to have collective gardens in Curitiba. And she brings the best seeds for her fellow gardeners and teaches them all the different ways to prepare the vegetables they grow. Manu organized a team of female chefs to prepare delicious food for the homeless in Curitiba. Above all, she cares for her family. Whenever we are abroad, she will always call her two daughters and husband to wish them a good night.

Long before I knew I would be a chef, I worked as a DJ in São Paulo's night scene. Remembering those crazy years, I suggest you turn your records on, play "She's a Sensation" by the Ramones, and prepare yourself for an incredible feast. In the following pages, you will enjoy Manu Buffara's stories and recipes for fantastic food. And you will leave the dance floor with a clean soul and a smile on your face.

Letter to My Younger Self

Some people want to be cooks, but they give up when they realize it's an unglamorous profession. Those who have a vocation for it remain in the field.

Know that many people will tell you no. Some will discourage you. There will be situations that will make you want to give up. But you shouldn't. Take advantage of these opportunities to prove you have the power to go far, show the world your beliefs and your roots, and view your profession from a unique perspective.

No one cook is the same as their colleagues. Each has a unique identity and is responsible for defining their style and establishing space within a team.

Becoming a respected professional requires humility above all, knowing that you are there to serve others. You won't leave school as a chef and run your own kitchen. You will wash a lot of salad, plates, and floors. With time and dedication, you become a good cook and professional and financial recognition will come. You will be a cook, as this will be your profession. The title of "chef" is a position.

Your professional fulfillment will not come overnight. It requires immense dedication, talent, and good teachers. The position of chef has something priestly about it because of the need for learning and because one has to earn their rank in the hierarchy.

Character and common sense are also essential in a professional career. Never copy the work of others. Recognize what they propose but prepare it your way. Those who understand what they are doing will succeed and impart that knowledge to others.

Your career will be shaped by the knowledge and experience gained throughout your journey.

Remember that it goes beyond vocation to have a passion for your work. Don't just pursue economic survival.

Creativity is undoubtedly one of the most valuable and interesting human qualities.

Creativity is the process of becoming sensitive to problems and gaps in knowledge, and disharmony. When you begin to explore what you don't know and stop exploring what you already know, you will feel closer to creating and believing in the power of your mind. Create something from nothing, take a chance, and make change.

— Manu

The fishing village of Ilha Rasa is a source of quality fish and seafood.

Welcome to Manu

I've wanted to be a creative chef since I was twenty-three years old. I wouldn't say that becoming one was easy. Life challenged me, distracted me, and tested my resolve at times. But I steeled myself to build a career abroad and commit to my dreams with my skills and financial limitations. I often revisited my notebooks, which mapped out the framework of my dream restaurant, and took stock of all the detailed considerations I had jotted down (page 95). It required commitment, dedication, and passion to make my dream come true.

In 2011, I opened Manu. And it was just the beginning. I needed to serve a lot of food before I was confident in my signature dishes and how I wanted to run my business. I also needed to give people time to understand my vision. In my experience, reality can sometimes be better than our wildest dreams. I am proud that I can wake up every morning to express my creativity.

This book is about my journey. It encapsulates all my ambitions, processes, and values through the years. With nearly two decades of experience in the industry, I can assure anyone that focus, resilience, and hard work can translate to success. Perhaps it seems like a long way off, but, in my case, I've managed to make it work by breaking it up into small journeys and setting achievable goals every day. Eventually, my attitude toward my dreams was the most crucial aspect in bringing them to fruition.

I was attracted to gastronomy and hospitality after I understood food's impact on one's state of mind. Here was an industry that would allow me to support others, shape the planet, and build stronger connections within my communities. My daily goal is to be the change I want for the world my daughters will live in.

This book contains a patchwork of essays that offers a glimpse into my story: my journey, with its genesis in Brazilian heritage; the people who've had the greatest impact on my career and success; the adversities that come with building a dream; and the guiding principles for my restaurant today. In fact, the title for each section of essays represents my culture, community, and identity. I've also presented four complete menu collections, bookended with the restaurant's customary welcome drinks and petit fours that respectively commence and conclude every meal.

I am proud to be a female chef at a time when we are more attuned to the needs of local food economies and communities. I feel I am helping to build a better world for the next generation. Thank you very much for your interest in my story and passion. I hope it inspires others to take the first step to achieving a dream.

(left) Melipona beehives mounted to the side of the restaurant; (right) a table set for dinner service.

(left) A table at the restaurant; (right) Manu and team members preparing for dinner service.

25

Araucaria

This evergreen, conferous pine is native to South America and the iconic city tree of Curitiba. It also symbolizes the roots of my story.

Local ingredients, kitchen routines, and tangerines

Cooking came to me as a calm love. I was eighteen and, having finished the first semester of my journalism studies in Brazil, had decided to spend my Brazilian summer holidays, working at a ski resort near Seattle, Washington. I wanted to improve my English and make some money. This is how I came to arrive in the quiet town of Snoqualmie in December 2001 during an unexpectedly mild season that saw very little snow. With few tourists, the ski resort had no part-time jobs for students such as me. There was, however, the fancy Salish Lodge & Spa, on the bank of the mighty Snoqualmie River. Without making an appointment, I went there and asked for a job. I was given a room-service position. After the first week, I was working double shifts, delivering food to guests in their rooms. I went above and beyond, for the best tips. My cart towels were always well ironed. I begged the kitchen for extra butter for the toast and fresh berries to embellish the pancakes and waffles. And I always put fresh flowers on the guests' trolleys. Eventually I was invited to be a kitchen assistant. My first assignment was a failure: tasked with deboning a chicken, I broke every single bone in the process. But, soon enough, I learned how to grill gourmet hamburgers and help prepare other elevated dishes.

I was making enough money to be financially independent, so I took a gap year from university, and my three-month work-holiday turned into two years. For the first year, I worked at the lodge, sleeping in a small staff bedroom, sharing a bathroom without a mirror, and even visiting food banks to get ingredients to prepare my meals off the job—I would do just about anything to make my money last longer. Then I spent a summer, with next to no money, hitching rides and camping in Alaska. I shared a truck bed with dozens of dogs on one long-haul trip, and I spent a month fishing halibut. I am proud of my skills scaling and gutting fish! And I can still remember finally rinsing my hair for the first time after being at sea for what seemed like ages.

I saved enough money to travel with a friend to Europe. When I called my mother to tell her I was in Paris, she didn't believe me. In 2003, without a laptop or smartphone, we planned our trips at libraries. We traveled to France, Slovenia, Slovakia, Hungary, Norway, Finland, Denmark, Belgium, Luxembourg, Spain, and Portugal. Our itineraries were built around free-entry days at the local museums. We slept in cheap hostels and saved money by eating at food trucks and carts, with the occasional nice meal as a treat. We spent Christmas in Budapest and New Year's Eve in Barcelona, then went to Portugal, where our money finally ran out. By my seventh month in Europe, my family was desperate to see me, and my father was happy to pay for my return ticket to Brazil.

Looking back now, everything makes sense. I couldn't be anywhere but at Manu. A good meal can shape people's state of mind, and I wanted to change the world with food. My experiences as a young adventurer eventually reconnected me to the kitchen, and to the ingredients that have always been present in my life. From my childhood spent near the fields and my father's work as a farmer to my mother's strong relationship with the sea—dating back to when her family lived in the port city of Paranaguá—the connection to my environment and surroundings has always been there.

When I returned to Brazil, I was different. I didn't fit into my previous life in Curitiba, and I no longer wanted to study journalism. I was hooked by hospitality: I believed in people and the good I could do by serving them, though I couldn't decide whether I wanted to run a kitchen or a hotel. Most of my family was skeptical about my new direction in life and encouraged me to finish the journalism course, in case my passion for cooking turned out to be just a summer love. But my mother understood that I had found my path and encouraged me.

I attended hospitality school and then culinary school, at Centro Europeu, in Curitiba. When I presented my final project, I was criticized for not making "real" dishes but a series of finger foods that would be better suited for magazine editorials than dinner plates. I had already established my way of thinking about menus, but I couldn't convince my teachers that this reflected a budding trend.

To earn money to return to Europe, I cooked for friends and family. Then, the generous support of my grandmothers made it possible for me to spend a year at the Italian Culinary Institute for Foreigners in Piedmont, Italy, where I learned techniques and kitchen routines. To acquire a good stage, you had to excel. I worked long hours, put up with many ill-tempered bosses, and kept tangerines in my bed to mask the smell of my male roommates.

My boss at Da Vittorio, a Michelin-starred restaurant near Bergamo, thought I had potential and occasionally offered me food magazines to read. One particular issue of *Apicius* featured an article on Noma. This restaurant focused on locality, seasonality, and sustainability and was inspired by the nature of cold Scandinavia and the wild ingredients of that part of the world. In 2006, I applied to work there, becoming one of the first international interns to work with René Redzepi's team in Copenhagen. But Denmark is an expensive country, and my money was running out. So I would wake up two hours before my shift in order to walk to the restaurant, and I'd have a sausage sandwich and a beer—the cheapest takeout 4 at convenience stores—every night on my way home. When my colleagues discovered how much walking I did every day, they got me an old bike.

At Noma, I was occasionally asked to explain the menu to Brazilian guests. On my final shift, I was informed that a Brazilian guest would be dining there that evening. To my astonishment, *I* was the guest—and was served an unforgettable meal. Typically, I do not like soft-boiled eggs, but I can still remember the incredible taste of the quail egg served at that dinner. Today, the freshness and simplicity of Noma's dishes frequently come to mind.

I took away two vital lessons from my five weeks at Noma. The first is to use the entire ingredient. (One day, I was about to throw out the top of a bell pepper, and the sous-chef asked me why someone from a country with so many starving people would discard that part of the vegetable.) The second is to forage ingredients in the wild—then to cook and serve them.

I could have built a successful career in Italy, but Curitiba called me back. The city believes in me and my wild ideas and big dreams. I belong to Curitiba, and I am happy here.

The patience in preparing bread over two days is what makes our brioche so special.

31

Turquoise floor and dry quark

For seven consecutive years of my childhood, Decembers were always the same. Early in the month, my mother would put my brother and me on a midnight bus from our home in Maringá and send us 265 miles (425 kilometers) southeast to Curitiba, to stay with my maternal grandparents. My brother—whose name is Eduardo, like my father and my father's father—and I started traveling by ourselves when he was six years old and I was eight. I still remember the way in which the bus company's name, Viação Garcia, was printed on the side of the big coach—the white letters, all in caps, painted on the soft blue finish. The typeface unified the legs of the As, making them look like inverted Vs. At 6 a.m., the bus would pull into the station, where Grandpa Nelson, with his warm smile and strong hands, was waiting for us. Our arrival in Curitiba signaled the start of my summer holidays, but it wasn't until I ran into my grandma's kitchen that my happiness was complete.

If I close my eyes, I can be easily transported to that enormous room, with its turquoise tile floor mirroring the waters of the nearby Atlantic Ocean. Curitiba is the capital of Paraná, a state in southern Brazil, close to Paraguay and Argentina. Unlike that of the hot and rainy Amazon forest or sunny Rio de Janeiro, the climate in Curitiba is mild. Some houses even have heating systems to combat the occasional harsh winter. My grandma's kitchen had an underfloor heating system, but it was never on during those hot Decembers.

Hot milk with molasses awaited us upon arrival, as did *pão na chapa*, a type of French toast made with a small baguette that we have only in Brazil. Grandma Lelia, whom we call Guegué, would press the bread with butter into a super-hot skillet, making sure both sides were golden, hot, and crunchy before serving it. For our welcome meal, Guegué would also serve a large dish of baked white taro (*inhame*) and sweet potatoes. I would drizzle them with a generous amount of molasses, which was always served on the side—for me, it was the ultimate mush-sugar combination. My brother would leave the table as soon as he had finished his meal, but I would remain, talking to my grandmother for what seemed like hours—about the bus trip, the rides on my horses, the family's rabbits, and recent adventures. And I would listen attentively as she shared her own childhood stories.

In the early mornings, Guegué's kitchen smelled of garlic and onions. The open kitchen was welcoming yet enormous, with enough space for eight people to work without bumping into one another. It was divided into two large working areas. The prep area was where the vegetables, herbs, fish, and meat were cleaned and chopped. The cooking area had a six-burner stove, a regular oven, a wood oven, and a barbecue. Both areas had a sink.

My grandfather's family is Lebanese, and sharing, abundance, and freshness were the rules of their kitchen. There was always good food waiting for us. I can recall, as if it was just yesterday, the scent of the sea breeze sweeping through that kitchen, especially during the weekends, as people came and went.

My grandma's parents were Italian. Grandma had married very young and learned a lot about cooking from her Lebanese mother-in-law, but after living many years by the sea, she also developed her own recipes. Her seafood dishes were especially scrumptious. My grandpa was responsible for bringing the best ingredients to every meal. Even though Curitiba was a thirty-minute drive to the sea, there was always fresh fish and shellfish at hand for Guegué's recipes.

My brother and I ate our breakfast at the rectangular wooden table that sat in the middle of the kitchen. I loved spending hours there in the quiet, once he had left the table, watching the food being made. In that kitchen, I saw milk being curdled and made into dry quark. My grandmother would leave a pan full of milk on the stove, the pan wrapped in a cheap wool blanket, something we referred to as *cobertor corta a febre* (meaning "blanket cuts the fever"). She still maintains that doing this keeps the milk at the right temperature, for the best curd.

Food was taken seriously in that house. The talented women who worked in that kitchen taught me to respect the ingredients and the time needed for each preparation. And that, to make food, we need good ingredients, dedication, patience, attention, and love. The most important ingredient in that kitchen was love. Everyone working there enjoyed what they were doing, cared about the preparation, and respected the essence of the ingredients, cooking, and eating together.

The araucaria tree, also known as the Brazilian pine, is the symbol of my home state, Paraná.

Mares, guava marmalade, and fruits from a tree

North Paraná's soil is reddish and impregnates the skin in a way that is hard to erase. Locals from that part of the state are known as *pé vermelho* (meaning "red foot") because of it. My father's family farm, Santa Helena, where my father still works to this day, is in North Paraná. We lived in nearby Maringá until I was fourteen years old, when we moved to Curitiba, in South Paraná.

While people from Curitiba tend to keep to themselves, *pé vermelho* are chatty and open to new friendships. It was easy to be happy in Maringá, especially when you were a curious and energetic child like I was. Maringá is a planned city with large streets, founded in 1947 in an area that was once part of the Atlantic Forest (*Mata Atlântica*), a biome extending down the Atlantic coast and 187 miles (300 kilometers) into the center of the country. And thanks to its proximity to some of the Atlantic Forest's conservation areas, Maringá has high quality, nutrient-rich soil for crops and is regarded as one of the greenest cities in Brazil. When last documented, in 2021, Maringá maintained one tree for every four inhabitants (meaning the number of trees in the city is equal to twenty-five per cent of the city's population), and it is one of the few cities in the country that manages to reconcile growth with environmental conservation.

As a child, I did a lot of outdoor activities, spending much of my time surrounded by animals. I had a peacock, chicken, rabbit, turtle, and fish at home, plus a few horses that my brother and I cared for on our family farm. I began horse-riding lessons at the age of three and participated in equestrian competitions for years, until I broke my collarbone as a teenager after falling off my horse.

Every winter, my paternal grandparents Eduardo and Maria Helena, both of Spanish ancestry, stayed at the farm. They always brought Araucaria seeds from Curitiba. Araucaria is an autochthonous pine from South America, and Curitiba's symbolic tree. Its seeds, hidden inside pine cones, are regarded around the world as an ancient food—pine nuts. Pine nuts have been an important part of Brazilian cuisine since they were cultivated, long before the Portuguese arrived in 1500. The Brazilian pine nut (*pinhão*) is much longer than those found in North America and Europe, about 2–3 inches (5–7.5 cm) in length, and a rich, dark brown color. When I was growing up, they were ubiquitous across the city during the Brazilian winter, and my grandparents would bring us lots. I had a small working kitchen with handmade pans in the backyard of the house at the family farm. I'd set a wood fire there and spend my mornings roasting and opening the Brazilian pine nuts that I would later serve to my family. I remember eating a significant amount of them before plating!

When I was young, I always looked forward to the weekends. I would wait, fully dressed, for my father to wake up at around 5 a.m., so that I could go with him to the farm, less than thirty minutes from our house in the city. I felt lucky to see the cows being milked. I remember how good it was to receive a glass of the milk, still warm and creamy. Then we would enjoy a long walk on the grounds.

I would harvest the carrots from the farm's vegetable gardens, and feed the horses and rabbits. I also loved checking the hens' nesting boxes for eggs, and to see the chicks hatching. I have wonderful memories of climbing trees and plucking fruits—jaboticaba, guava, acerola, and mango—right off the branches. I was a fearless child. When it was difficult to find a starting point to climb a tree, I would lead my mare Donatela, or perhaps Alvorada (a horse blind in one eye), under the branch for a boost up. I also spent some afternoons at the farmhouse kitchen with Elaine, the farmhand, preparing amazing butter and cream.

I would bring the weekend's harvest from the farm back to Maringá and proudly deliver them to Claudete, the cook at our home. She was a tall brunette who had no time for jokes, and her cooking was incredible. I still remember the aroma of her pancakes fresh out of the oven. Our open kitchen had a six-seat rectangular table in its center, with long benches on either side where my brother and I sat while she toasted bread with butter in an old, heavy skillet with wooden handles. She would serve us this or a piece of cake in the afternoons; I enjoyed dipping it, still warm, into a glass of milk. Occasionally, I set up a table in front of our Maringá house to sell homemade juices, ice cream, and banana cake made by Claudete.

When the school day ended, I often had a quick snack of bread and ice cream at the Café Cremoso bakery, still operating in Maringá today. Other times, I prepared this snack in our kitchen once my father arrived home with fresh bread from the bakery—even though Claudete would scold me, saying it would give me indigestion. I never felt ill after having it with milk, drunk directly from the bottle.

To this day, one of my favorite activities is spending time with my father at his farm. I inherited from him a laidback way of viewing the world. Like him, I do not waste time complaining about life. I'm very hands-on, and I always problem-solve. My hardworking father doesn't do small talk, and I enjoy connecting to this side of my personality when we are together. He is a dedicated family man and makes every effort to ensure I, my friends, and my girls are happy when we visit Santa Helena.

Not too long ago, I decided to make guava marmalade with the abundance of fresh fruit my friends' children and I plucked from the trees. I planned to let it cure overnight on the stove over very low heat, as I do at the restaurant. When I left the kitchen, my father, aware of my intention, kept vigil over the stockpot until I returned the following morning. He said he was afraid something might happen with the kitchen's wooden ceiling. We made a huge amount of guava marmalade. As I transferred it into jars, my heart warmed with each spoonful, thinking of my beloved father in the kitchen taking care of the marmalade while I slept.

The native Brazilian jaboticaba tree with fruit, like the ones my father had on his farm in Maringá.

We eat with our eyes first. At Manu, attention is given to everything, including our dishware.

Saturday lunch, market trips, and shopping bags

Every Friday in the late 1990s, I would call my maternal grandmother, Guegué, and ask her about Saturday's lunch menu. If she answered "fish" or "Lebanese food," I'd cancel everything a teenager like me would be up to, put on a lovely dress, and do my hair—I had to look my best to go to my grandparents' place. After all, the rewards of Guegué's big smile and affectionate hug, the happy atmosphere, and excellent food were guaranteed. Saturday lunch was a big event at my grandparents' house, and I'd arrive at their spacious and bright apartment at noon sharp. Each of their six sons and daughters would come with their partners, and all twelve grandsons were also invited. Sometimes, I brought along a boyfriend or a friend. And I had only one piece of advice for them: "Never leave anything on the plate."

The adults sat at the large circular dining table, while we teenagers sat at a table in the adjoining room. I loved to help Guegué with the lunch preparation, and I was particularly fond of setting the tables. She traveled frequently and often returned home with new tablecloths and napkins. Sometimes she took me to Curitiba's city center to buy sets from a Portuguese woman who hand-embroidered the tablecloths. Guegué was partial to the white ones with tiny, colorful flowers.

An hour before the meal was to be served, she might gently say, "Manoella, bring me the blue tablecloth." I would pull open the heavy wooden drawer of the buffet and take out the perfectly ironed tablecloth and its matching napkins. I still remember how they smelled. Together, we chose the napkin rings that would best complement the crystal glasses and the dining set being used for that meal. I loved all the details—the proper place for the dessert spoon and fork (just above the plates), and the different glasses for red and white wine (plus a bigger water glass). After setting the table for the adults, we would take care of the setting for the kids. Guegué had colorful glasses for the younger dinner guests, and she allowed me to decide which my cousins and I would use. I felt so special.

Grandpa Nelson would come to the teenagers' table to inspect the dishes at the end of the meal. He commanded respect, and his grandchildren and grandchildren's friends always polished off their plates; otherwise, they'd have to eat all the left-over rice. (My grandfather grew up during wartime and would not accept food waste.) Truthfully, the food was so good, there was rarely anything left on our plates.

From time to time, Grandpa Nelson invited me to go shopping with him. I looked forward to those outings. He was well known in Curitiba's markets and the vendors loved him. Whenever I tell an elderly vendor that I'm his granddaughter, they launch into a good story about him or tell me about the advice he gave them to improve sales, such as having cut fruit on display for shoppers to see how good it is inside. He was a picky customer who liked to sample the fruits and vegetables on offer. He never waited for an invitation; instead, he would grab the one he wanted most, clean it with his handkerchief, and take a bite. We would feel the weight of the silence before his verdict was handed down. "Very good! Please make seven packages of these," he would say if he had enjoyed it. His order could mean the best sale of the day. When he found something delicious, he would buy some for his six sons and daughters to enjoy at their homes. All of them knew that every Saturday, lined up on the floor in Guegué's kitchen, shopping bags with the town's best and most exotic fruits and veggies were waiting for them to take home. It was amazing to shop for that produce, but it was even better to have it waiting for us in that kitchen. I always looked forward to opening the bag when we arrived home with it after Saturday lunch.

It was in my grandparents' house that I came to love seafood. My grandmother had the best recipes and used only fresh ingredients. She especially loved shrimp (prawns). Her shrimp with chayote, shrimp cocktail, fried fish with shrimp and okra, shrimp dumplings, and shrimp pie were all classics. She had an unforgettable recipe of anchovies with dates, and she still makes the family's best *moqueca* (a traditional Brazilian stew of fish and shellfish). She was also a huge fan of intricate recipes. For stuffed eggs, she'd have her team of kitchen assistants replace the cooked yolks with fish cream or mullet roe. Dozens of dishes—with a variety of aromas, colors, flavors, and textures—were arranged on a sideboard near the dining table. And we always saved room for desserts, which never disappointed, especially when they involved bananas.

After a few drinks, the grown-ups would grow nostalgic and talk about the children's exploits. More often than not, one of them would bring up the day I fell into the swimming pool, when I was just four. We were at my father's farm, and there was no one watching over me. Soaking wet, I walked into the house and declared, "I saved myself." Guegué and my mom like to say they are proud that I continue to find ways to save myself to this day.

Grandpa Nelson did not like the idea of me becoming a chef. In his eyes, I was too clever to make a living cooking for strangers. Guegué was also worried when I decided to open Manu. She thought it could be too big a step. But she adopted a positive attitude, and according to her, I never lacked courage, perseverance, or resilience. She frequently draws similarities between me and Grandpa Nelson: our curiosity about new things, our ease in talking to people from all walks of life, and our appreciation for the simple things. Grandpa Nelson enjoyed humble places, people, and home-cooked food, but he could adapt to any environment. And Guegué believed that I would have a bright future, like him. I agreed with her, but I also like to think that I took from her the importance of a beautiful table setting, and of always receiving guests with a smile.

Hard work, independence, and comfort food

My parents divorced when I was fourteen, and my mom and us children moved to Curitiba. She worked hard, and took care with what we ate. Fresh fruits and vegetables were always a part of our meals. I can still clearly picture the first beef stroganoff she prepared for a Sunday lunch. This classic Russian dish is popular in Brazil, and my mother's recipe takes hours to prepare. She is discerning with the ingredients and has special pots for each stage of its preparation. That Sunday, the beef was chopped into uniform cubes and then slow-cooked, the excess meat juice ladled into a bowl. She seasoned the meat with plenty of whiskey and carefully selected the mushrooms to add to the dish. The onion was cut with uniform precision. And the accompanying rice was fluffy and super aromatic. When the three of us sat down at the table for lunch in our new home in Curitiba, I understood things had changed. And that my mother, through her home cooking, was telling us that we could count on her.

My mother and I have different attitudes toward life. She doesn't approve of my footwear choices nor of the trendy cutlery and crockery I put on the table for Sunday lunches. She is traditional. But it is her food that I crave when I'm feeling tired or sad. And she is always ready to come over to prepare the dish I want. My mom makes a crab dish with eggs that I sometimes dream about. When I have special guests for Sunday lunch, I summon my mother to make the dessert. She always has an amazing, and comforting, recipe to serve the guests. She loves to travel and often took my brother and me to the places she visited. And she saved money to take me to the best restaurant in town, just so I could try the tasting menu. I remember how happy she was after seeing me in a team photo from Guido Restaurant in Piedmont, Italy, where I worked as an intern. She is always proud whenever I receive an invitation to cook at a top restaurant, wherever it is in the world.

I learned from my mother to be an independent woman, to value my career, to finish what I start, and to take good care of my girls and husband. I inherited from her my soft heart, my mania for organization, and my curiosity for other cultures. Like her, I am happiest near the sea and annoyed when the silver is incorrectly positioned at a table setting.

If there's a spice missing from a dish at Manu, I'll notice it. My team is amazed that I can notice when even a pinch of cinnamon, a hint of cumin, or a drop of lime juice was omitted in the preparation of a recipe—and that I can name the missing ingredient. Every ingredient in a recipe serves a purpose. And the order in which they are used impacts the taste of the dish. I am grateful to my mother for teaching me that.

Love, career, and sheep brains

The year was 2004; the day was May 7; the occasion was my twenty-first birthday, and I was hanging out with friends. That's when I met Dario. We got along well from the start, but I had already booked my trip to Italy. I informed him that in four months I would be leaving for a year-long culinary course. He laughed at me, saying that it was just a kiss and not a marriage proposal. Destiny knew this was a futile conversation because we had already forged a strong bond. I left Curitiba dating my future husband. We maintained a long-distance relationship through seemingly endless telephone calls and love letters. I must be as crazy as people say I am, because I had a *D* for Dario tattooed on my left arm during that time. When I received my diploma, he met me in Milan so we could travel. Our forty-day itinerary included stops in Italy and Morocco.

Dario likes to say he immediately recognized how my time spent in Italy turned me into an even better cook and changed the course of my life as I became entirely food-oriented. From then on, trip planning involved researching the locale's best food markets and the best places for home-style dishes and chef-led menus. Fortunately, Dario began to enjoy the culinary scene too. A few years later, Dario, who runs his own law firm, learned the basics of cooking at Centro Europeu, where I was teaching. He understands cooking and makes the best barbecue ever—nobody prepares chicken heart like he does. He often recalls when he hunted for truffles with our friend and truffle hunter Giorgio and then tasted the freshly grated *tartufo* on *carne cruda* (a typical Italian raw meat dish). He was captivated by Italian food and deeply respected the Italian attitude toward ingredients and seasonality. We exchanged our vows on November 23, 2012, in a ceremony by the sea in Punta del Este, Uruguay.

Dario and I achieved even greater synchronicity after traveling together. I brought adventure and spontaneity to his life, and he organized our daily routines and supported us as a couple in every way imaginable. Today, he tests all my menus and brings a fresh viewpoint to every dish. He is also the best father to my girls. Because he stays home with them, I can travel the world to cook and talk about the food I make. When I am abroad, he will study online videos in order to perfect the girls' ponytails before school. We make a good team and follow our mantra: Let's be the change.

During a trip to Marrakesh in 2006, I insisted on trying lamb brain in Jemaa El-Fna, Morocco's largest open market and one of the best places to eat this specialty. Dario had been avoiding it for the entire trip. It was nearly dusk yet still hot when we arrived at the market, which was swarming with people. The heart of the old medina transformed before our eyes as food vendors set up their stalls. There was movement in every direction and a cacophony of sounds—shouting, clattering pots and pans, the roaring of motorcycle engines. Smoky steam danced in the air. Next to one bench occupied by locals were several stewed sheep heads. The contents of the vendor's stockpot were bubbling away. Dario nearly fled.

The brains were simmered in a flavorful broth, resulting in a soft and unctuous texture. While I am not squeamish when it comes to food, I cannot say I liked it. Still, I refused to budge and ate almost the entire portion. To be truly experienced, a chef needs to be gutsy.

I was sick for three days. Dario ended up visiting Madrid by himself.

An open fire for roasting corn and making molasses and sugar at Cerro Azul.

41

Vegetables are an essential part of a Manu menu, and we reflect the best versions of them.

Tattoos, whiskey, and craftsmen

If you come to my house and turn over some of my decorative objects, you will see them labeled with a place name and year. I like to bring back souvenirs from my travels and, being ultra-organized, I add a note to each piece to record the place of origin and year it was acquired. My souvenirs include three wooden ducks with metal heads from a 2017 trip to Vienna, an antique candle holder from a 2018 trip to Lyon, a collection of miniature stone houses found in Istanbul in 2019, and a fur rug from an antique shop in Amsterdam in 2020.

One of my most treasured pieces is a leather aviator bag that belonged to my paternal grandfather, Eduardo. It sits under a round dark wooden table in the entrance hall of my home. When my widowed grandmother Maria Helena died, my family had to empty her apartment. I wanted some special items as keepsakes, and when I came across Eduardo's suitcase, I felt like I'd won a prize. He had been a pilot and had inspired the two wings and the monogram "ER" that's tattooed on my right arm. For years, he carried that bag to work. It made a metallic *click* when he closed it, and I would wonder what was inside.

I was very close to Eduardo and Maria Helena. Since both my parents worked outside the home, my grandparents would often take me to my show-jumping events, supporting me from the sidelines. When I was twelve, they drove me to São Paulo for a tournament in which I won first prize, a moment immortalized in a photograph of them standing at my side that I keep in my office. They were also the ones who dropped me off at soccer games when I was seventeen. The rest of my family supported Curitiba, but I was all for the rival team, Athletico Paranaense. I went to those games alone, and they would pick me up afterward.

When I decided to open my restaurant, Eduardo was retired and had passed down the farm to my father to manage. He was one of the first visitors to the property of my future restaurant, and he was there every day to monitor the restaurant's construction. He was eighty at the time and loved his whiskey. He would drink from a stainless-steel hip flask while the builders transformed 317 Dom Pedro II Street into Manu. He also knew the best carpenter to hire and the cheapest places to buy the best-quality materials. As he was frugal and hated the idea of wasting money, he would insist I drive miles to get a bargain. If I couldn't go, he would send someone else.

Eduardo also knew the best leather craftsmen in town and had the leather handles of our first meat knives at the restaurant engraved with Manu's logo and opening date: January 6, 2011. This day coincides with the Christian Feast of the Epiphany, which marks the end of Christmas festivities and celebrates the visit of the Magi to the Christ Child. On each anniversary of this day, I think of Grandpa Eduardo being by my side. He passed away, and I no longer use those knives at the restaurant. Instead, I keep them at home, to use on special occasions.

Grandpa Eduardo was one of my most loyal customers and often brought friends along, introducing them to my food. In 2020, Manu underwent a renovation. Inspired by the knives Eduardo had had engraved, I ordered as a tribute to him a set from Aloisio Selhorst. His unique, handcrafted knives are made with carbon-steel laminate and noble wooden handles, secured with stainless-steel pins. It is a special moment when each person at the table selects from an option of five handmade knives which knife they will use to cut the meat, which is often one of the last dishes on Manu's menu. My eyes will well up with tears when I see a customer choosing one of those beautiful knives. I take a minute of silence to honor my dear and ever-present grandfather.

The Guaraqueçaba Environmental Protection Area is protected land located on the coast of Paraná.

45

Drinks

All Manu tasting menus start with a fermented drink made in-house. I came up with this idea when I had been reading old publications for research. We use regional fruits and vegetables to make the fermented concoctions, which include kombuchas. The team and I have good fun creating them.

(left to right) Fermented jaboticaba (page 50), fermented grape and beet (page 51), and fermented sweet potato, chile, and passion fruit (page 49).

Fermented sweet potato, chile, and passion fruit

This is my favorite welcome drink. The sweet potato and passion fruit we use come from the same farm. So it was inevitable that I pair them to produce this fermented drink.

Serves 4

For the ginger bug	100 g grated organic ginger
	300 ml water
	15 g sugar

For the spice infusion	1 g grated dried galangal
	0.5 g grated nutmeg
	500 ml water

For the fermented sweet potato	300 g sweet potato
	60 ml lemon juice
	50 g pimenta de cheiro (green chile pepper)
	500 ml Spice Infusion (see above)
	180 g sugar
	180 g fresh passion fruit pulp
	1.5 L water
	50 ml Ginger Bug (see above)

Ginger bug Place the ginger in a canning jar. Add the water and sugar and mix well. Cover and leave at room temperature. Open the jar 3–4 times a day, letting the oxygen replenish for 30 seconds each time, then cover it and shake well. Repeat this process for 3–5 days, until the mixture is bubbling. Store in the refrigerator.

Spice infusion In a small saucepan, combine the spices with 250 ml of water. Bring to a boil over medium heat. Boil for 2 minutes. Remove the pan from the heat, cover, and infuse for 15 minutes. Stir in the remaining 250 ml of water.

Fermented sweet potato Grate the unpeeled sweet potato on a coarse grater. Rinse under cold running water for 20 seconds to remove some of the starch. Place in a bowl and mix with the lemon juice. Reserve. Using a mortar and pestle, crush the chile lightly to extract the flavor. Mix the chile with the sweet potato. Combine the spice infusion, sugar, and passion fruit pulp in a blender, blending for 3 minutes on high speed to dissolve the sugar and oxygenate the mixture. Place the sweet potato mixture in a large glass jar suitable for fermentation and cover with the blended mixture. Add the water and mix well. Finally, add the ginger bug and stir again. Cover the jar with a cloth or cheesecloth (muslin) and let it ferment at room temperature in a dark place for 3–5 days, until small bubbles form—the time will vary depending on the room's temperature.

Once the liquid is bubbling, it's ready for the second fermentation. Strain the mixture through a chinois. Pour the mix into a plastic bottle, filling two-thirds of the container and leaving a third free as headspace. Let it ferment for 3–8 days, until the bottle is bloated (due to the production of carbon dioxide). Once fermented, store in the refrigerator until needed. Be careful when opening for the first time—the second fermentation will have produced gas pressure.

Fermented jaboticaba

Jaboticaba is a sweet white fruit with a dark skin that's full of flavor. We discovered that the dark skin is actually a deep magenta, which adds extraordinary flavor and a pink tint to concoctions. Although it is difficult to find at markets, it's often found growing wild in backyards, in many Brazilian states.

Serves 4

For the spice syrup	100 g sugar
	100 ml water
	10 g black lemon
	1 clove
	1 star anise

For the fermented jaboticaba	1 kg jaboticabas
	20 g sugar
	1 g fleur de sel
	700 ml water
	100 ml Spice Syrup (see above)
	60 ml lemon juice

Spice syrup Combine the sugar and water in a saucepan. Grate the black lemon into the pan. Add the clove and star anise. Bring the mixture to a boil and boil until it becomes a thin syrup. Remove from the heat, cover, and set aside for at least 2 hours, until cool.

Fermented Jaboticaba Place the jaboticabas in a bowl and mash with your hands to break the skin and release some of the juice. Add 10 g of sugar and the fleur de sel and continue to mix with your hands. Pour the mixture into a glass pitcher (jug) and add the water, spice syrup, and lemon juice. Cover the pitcher with cheesecloth (muslin) and tie it tightly. Ferment for 1–4 days, at room temperature, until the mixture is acidic, with a slightly vinegary aroma—the time will vary depending on the room's temperature.

Strain the mixture through a chinois into a bowl, add the remaining 10 g of sugar, and stir well. Pour the mixture into a plastic bottle, filling two-thirds of the container and leaving a third free as headspace. Ferment for 2–5 days, until the bottle is bloated (due to the production of carbon dioxide). Store in the refrigerator until needed.

Note: Be careful when opening for the first time—the second fermentation will have produced gas pressure.

Fermented grape and beet

Italian immigrants brought grape fermentation to the south of Brazil. In this preparation, I use the original production method and add jambu, a herb found in many dishes from north Brazil. I like to serve it cold.

Serves 4

For the jambu flower yeast	10 g jambu flower
	200 ml room-temperature water
	10 g sugar
For the fermented grapes	1 kg red globe grapes
	160 g sugar
	1 g fleur de sel
	500 ml beet (beetroot) juice
	500 ml water
	50 ml Jambu Flower Yeast
	(see above)

Jambu flower yeast Place the jambu flowers in a plastic bottle, filling a third of the container. In a small bowl, combine the water and the sugar and stir until dissolved. Pour into the container, completely submerging the flowers.

Cover, then set aside at room temperature for at least 3 days, opening the bottle for up to 30 seconds 2–3 times each day, until the mixture ferments and the solution is bubbling. Transfer the bottle to the refrigerator.

Fermented grapes Place the grapes in a bowl. Using your hands or a pestle and mortar, mash them to break up the skins and release some of the juice. Add 150 g of sugar and fleur de sel and mix.

Pour the mixture into a glass pitcher (jug) and top with the beet (beetroot) juice and water. Add the jambu flower yeast and mix well. Cover the pitcher with cheesecloth (muslin) and tie it tightly. Ferment at room temperature for 1–4 days, until the mixture is acidic and the aroma has changed (it will smell sour).

Strain the mixture through a chinois into a bowl, add the remaining 10 g of sugar, and stir well. Pour the liquid into a plastic bottle, filling two-thirds of the container and leaving a third free as headspace. Let it ferment for 2–5 days, until the bottle is bloated (due to the production of carbon dioxide). Store in the refrigerator until needed. Be careful when opening for the first time—the second fermentation will have produced gas pressure.

Metamorphosis

This is the complete change of form, nature, or structure—a transformation or transmutation. We are not the same as before; we change every moment. Metamorphosis is evolution without loss; it is about flight and maturity.

Scallop, cashew nut milk, and native honey

In my opinion, emerina honey, which originates in Paraná, is at the top of the honey chain. A rare honey of unparalleled complexity, it has very low sweetness and high acidity. Its taste is intriguing, with characteristics of lemon, resin, and truffles.

Serves 4

For the scallops	Cashew Nut Oil (see page 142), for greasing
	120 g fresh scallops (about 8)
For the cashew nut milk	150 g cashew nuts
	200 ml whole (full-fat) milk
	25 ml rice vinegar
	4 g salt
For the native honey vinaigrette	50 ml emerina native bee honey
	25 ml Cashew Nut Oil (see page 142)
To serve	1 g fleur de sel
	6 g dill
	2 g purple oxalis sprouts

Scallops — Grease a sheet of parchment paper with cashew nut oil. Thinly slice the scallops into disks.

Cashew nut milk — In a Thermomix, combine the cashews and milk and mix until smooth and creamy. Transfer the nut milk to a bowl, add the vinegar, and season with salt. Set aside to cool.

Native honey vinaigrette — In a bowl, mix the emerina honey and cashew nut oil but do not emulsify.

To serve — Drizzle the scallops with the native honey vinaigrette. Divide the scallops among the plates. Cover with 50 ml of cashew nut milk. Finish with the fleur de sel, dill, and oxalis sprouts.

Sea bass, mushrooms, and cucumbers

I remember as a child shedding tears over the immensity, beauty, and strength of the sea. It continues to inspire and relax me and cleanse my soul.

Serves 4

For the mushroom salsa Part 1	400 g shimeji mushrooms 200 g shiitake mushrooms 750 ml water 12 ml vegetarian oyster sauce
Part 2	10 g hydrated tapioca flour 25 ml clear soy sauce 25 ml rice vinegar
For the palm heart vinaigrette	75 ml Palm Heart Sauce (see page 154) 10 ml rice vinegar 10 ml tucupí
For the cured sea bass	2 g fine pink salt 2 g sugar 1 x 200 g cleaned sea bass fillet olive oil, for greasing
For the pickled onion	100 ml rice vinegar 50 g sugar 100 g onion, julienned
For the charred cucumber	150 g Japanese cucumber 10 ml olive oil 3 g fleur de sel
To serve	30 g chopped chives 4 physalis, sliced (optional) 2 g Mushroom Powder (see page 206)

Mushroom salsa Part 1 Preheat the oven to 175°F (80°C). Arrange the mushrooms on a Silpat and bake for 3–4 hours, stirring occasionally, until the mushrooms are dehydrated. Transfer the mushrooms to a saucepan. With 200 ml of water, deglaze the Silpat, scraping well with a spoon to extract all the flavors.

Pour this water into the pan with the mushrooms, add 550 ml of water and the vegetarian oyster sauce, and cook over low heat for 1 hour. Remove from the heat and cover the pan. Infuse overnight.

The next day, put the pan over medium heat again and cook until the mushroom stock has reduced to 250 ml. Strain and set aside to cool at room temperature.

Part 2 Dissolve the hydrated tapioca flour in 50 ml of room temperature mushroom stock, then set aside. Pour the remaining 200 ml of mushroom stock into a saucepan and bring to a boil over medium heat. Add the soy sauce and vinegar. Boil for 5 minutes, then whisk in the dissolved tapioca and its soaking liquid. Cook for another 2–5 minutes, on medium heat, until the sauce thickens. Set aside until needed.

Palm heart vinaigrette With an immersion blender, blend all the ingredients in a large bowl. Set aside until needed.

Cured sea bass Combine the salt and sugar in a small bowl. Sprinkle the mixture all over the sea bass fillet. Place the fillet on a wire rack set on a rimmed baking sheet and refrigerate for 12 hours to cure.

Once cured, pat dry the fillet with paper towel. Cut the fillet into ¼-inch (5-mm) slices and place between 2 sheets of parchment paper greased with olive oil until needed.

Pickled onion Put the vinegar and sugar in a saucepan and bring to a boil until the sugar is fully dissolved. Remove from the heat and let cool. Once cooled, place the mixture in a container and submerge the onion in the liquid. Refrigerate for at least 2 days before serving.

Charred cucumber Preheat a grill to medium (300°F/150°C).

Trim the ends of the cucumber and peel. Cut in half lengthwise and scrape out the seeds using a spoon. Cut the cucumber in half crosswise, and then each in half crosswise again. Cut the cucumber into sticks and place them on the hot grill for 1 minute on each side.

To serve Scoop 50 ml of mushroom salsa into each deep dish. Arrange a row of folded sea bass slices in the center. Spoon a little palm heart vinaigrette around the dish. Arrange the pickled onion on the sea bass.

Cut the cucumber into ½-inch (1-cm) pieces and season with olive oil and fleur de sel. Arrange overtop the fish. Sprinkle with the chives, then garnish with 2 slices of physalis, if using. Finish with a sprinkling of the mushroom powder. Serve immediately.

Slipper lobster, chicken liver, rump steak fat

Every Christmas, I make this liver pâté for the family dinner. I especially like it when this pâté, which combines chicken liver with cumin and peppers, touches any kind of seafood in the same bite. When I first prepared the slipper lobster for this recipe, I roasted it slightly, and I knew immediately that I would pair it with chicken liver pâté.

When creating a dish, I will often close my eyes, remain silent, and wait to be inspired by what is missing in the preparation. After pairing the slipper lobster and pâté, rump steak fat came to mind—the pinnacle moment of a Brazilian barbecue is the serving of the rump steak, which always has a layer of delicious fat. I prepared this recipe again, adding rump steak, and then closed my eyes. The acidity was missing. So I introduced apple tartare with lemon zest to the plate.

Serves 4

For the chicken liver pâté Part 1	100 g fresh chicken livers
	20 g butter
	20 g onion, brunoise
	5 g pimenta de cheiro (green chile pepper), brunoise
	2 g white pepper
	50 ml cognac
	100 ml heavy (double) cream
	75 ml whole (full-fat) milk
	45 g egg yolks (about 2 eggs)
Part 2	3 g ground cumin
	2 g green peppercorns
	1 g ground cinnamon
	5 g salt
For the green apple tartare	100 g green apple
	juice of 1 lime
	zest of 1 lemon
	1 g salt
	1 g black pepper
	15 ml olive oil
For the rump steak fat	100 g rump steak fat
	2 g salt
	10 g sliced scallion (spring onion)
For the slipper lobster	4 x 1 kg fresh slipper lobsters
	25 g sugar
	25 g fine pink salt
	15 ml olive oil
	30 g brown butter (beurre noisette)
To serve	1 radish, thinly sliced

Chicken liver pâté

Part 1 Clean the livers, then immediately freeze them for 6 hours.

Heat a skillet over high heat. Add 10 g of butter and the livers, searing each side for 30 seconds. Set aside. Add the remaining 10 g of butter to the hot pan. Add the onion and sauté for 12 minutes, or until golden. Stir in the chile and white pepper and sauté until fragrant.

Add the cognac and flambé until reduced by half. Stir in the cream and bring to a boil. Immediately remove from the heat and transfer to a blender. Add the liver and blend on high speed, gradually adding the milk until the mixture drops to a temperature of 104°F (40°C). Add the egg yolks, one at a time, beating constantly.

Preheat the oven to 194°F (90°C). Pour the mixture in a terrine and cover with aluminum foil. Bake in a bain-marie in the oven for 1 hour. Transfer the liver mixture to the refrigerator to cool down.

Part 2 Put the liver mixture in a blender and blend until smooth. Add the cumin, green peppercorns, and cinnamon and blend on high speed for 5 minutes. Season with salt and set aside until needed.

Green apple tartare Cut the apple in brunoise. Combine the apple and lime juice in a small bowl. Add the lemon zest, salt, pepper, and olive oil and mix well.

Rump steak fat Preheat a skillet over medium-high heat. Cut the rump steak fat into small equal pieces. Fry in the skillet until rendered. Pass the fat through a sieve, then stir in the salt. Let cool. Stir in the scallion (spring onion) and set aside.

Slipper lobster Remove the shells from the lobsters and keep the tails intact. Dry the lobster meat with paper towel. Combine the sugar and salt in a small bowl, then sprinkle all over the lobsters.

Place them on a wire rack set over a baking sheet and refrigerate for 8 hours.

When ready to serve, preheat a skillet to medium heat. Add the olive oil and slipper lobsters and cook for 1 minute on each side. Drizzle with hot brown butter (beurre noisette).

To serve Scoop a spoonful of pâté onto each plate, spreading it out with the back of the spoon. Using a kitchen torch, lightly toast the pâté. Put some apple tartare in the center. Place a hot lobster overtop the apple tartare, drizzle with the rump steak fat, and top with radish slices. Serve immediately.

Black squid, corn, and cashew nuts

Thoughts, ideas, angles, points—there are many ways to create. It all depends on how you will use the creation. Making a dish with squid was something I always wanted to do. During squid season, they arrive at Manu practically still alive. I wanted a dish that would be worthy of the squid's death. And so came the perfect combination of lightly braised squid and sour corn with squid ink vinaigrette.

Serves 4

For the sour cream of corn	35 g butter
	20 g onion, brunoise
	350 g corn kernels
	180 ml whole (full-fat) milk
	25 ml lemon juice
	8 g salt
For the crunchy cashews	100 g cashew nuts
	2 g Italian parsley leaves
	40 g butter
	zest of 2 lemons
	5 g salt
For the squid	200 g fresh and clean squid
	2 L water
For the squid ink vinaigrette	15 g white miso paste
	10 ml balsamic vinegar
	7 ml sunflower oil
	5 ml squid ink
	5 ml emerina native bee honey
	5 ml balsamic cream
To serve	20 g brown butter (beurre noisette)
	5 g fleur de sel
	8 g micro basil leaves

Sour cream of corn Melt the butter in a skillet over medium heat. Add the onion and sauté for 12 minutes. Add the corn and sauté for 10 minutes on low heat. Pour in the milk, increase heat to medium, and gently simmer for 30 minutes, or until the corn is soft and cooked through. Transfer to a Thermomix and mix on high speed until a smooth and homogeneous cream. If necessary, pass through a sieve to remove the skins from the corn. Let cool, then season with lemon juice and salt.

Crunchy cashews Coarsely chop the cashews. Chiffonade the parsley. Set aside both.

Heat the butter in a skillet over medium-low heat, until lightly browned. Add the cashews and cook until golden. Remove from the heat. Mix well, then let cool. Stir in the lemon zest, chopped parsley, and salt.

Squid Cut the squid into 2-inch (5-cm) squares. Make 1/16-inch (2-mm) crosshatch pattern cuts on the inside of the squid.

Bring the water to a boil. Add the squid and blanch for 10 seconds. Drain, then transfer to a large bowl of ice water for 2 minutes. Drain again.

Squid ink vinaigrette Blend all the ingredients in a blender until well combined.

To serve Heat the cream of corn. In a skillet, quickly sauté the squid in the brown butter (beurre noisette) over medium-low heat. Using a kitchen torch, lightly char the squid until golden. Add half the squid ink vinaigrette and stir well.

Pour 100 g of sour cream of corn into each deep dish. Sprinkle over the crunchy cashews. Divide the squid among the dishes and drizzle with the squid ink vinaigrette. Finish with the fleur de sel and basil leaves.

Beet and bottarga

I've worked with beets (beetroots) many times. They always come in different sizes and shapes. This recipe is best made with a ruby queen beet harvested on a full moon, at its sweetest. I like to bake them because of the caramelization.

Serves 4

For the beets	100 g medium organic beets (beetroots)
	250 ml beet (beetroot) juice
	50 ml tucupi
	30 ml cranberry juice
	30 ml fish sauce (*nam pla*)
	20 ml light soy sauce
	10 ml rice vinegar
	10 g black garlic
	25 g cubed cold butter
	1 g hydrated tapioca flour
For the bottarga	10 ml olive oil
	60 g bottarga
To serve	3 g fleur de sel

Beets Preheat a combination oven to 350°F (180°C) with 50% humidity. Roast the whole unpeeled beets (beetroots) for 40 minutes, or until tender. Let cool, then peel.

Cold-smoke the beets for 10 minutes. Cut each in half and set aside.

In a skillet, combine 230 ml of beet juice, tucupi, cranberry juice, fish sauce, soy sauce, vinegar, and black garlic and boil over medium heat for 25 minutes, or until reduced by half. Transfer the mixture to a blender and blend well. Strain through a sieve back into the skillet and bring to a boil. Add the butter little by little, tilting the skillet in a circular motion until incorporated and emulsified. Add the beets and cook over low heat for 2 minutes.

Combine the remaining 20 ml of beet juice and tapioca flour in a small bowl. Add to the beet mixture and cook for 1 minute, or until the sauce has slightly thickened.

Bottarga Heat a nonstick skillet over medium heat. Add the olive oil and bottarga. Cook the bottarga for 2 minutes on each side. Transfer to a plate to cool. Once cool, place the bottarga in a food processor and process until fine.

To serve Heat the beets in their sauce in a small skillet over medium heat until hot. Place half a beet on each plate and top with beet sauce. Finish with the bottarga and fleur de sel.

White mussels, turnip, and chile

Every time I eat a turnip I am intrigued by the layers of flavor. I wanted to extract the best of turnips in this recipe, so I combined them with yogurt and soy sauce, then added the white mussels and tucupi to boost the umami. After I served this dish, my fish suppliers asked where I was sourcing the white mussels I wanted, because they couldn't guarantee they would be white. Only Geovane of Inácio Pescados, one of my fish suppliers, knew about this special kind of white mussel from Brazil's southern coast (page 108).

Serves 4

For the turnips	250 g white lady turnips
	90 ml water
	85 g plain (natural) yogurt
	15 ml light soy sauce
For the white mussels	12 white mussels
	25 g brown butter (beurre noisette)
	100 ml tucupi
For the chiles	40 g pimenta de cheiro (green chile pepper)
	15 g white onion, brunoise
	10 ml olive oil
	5 ml rice vinegar
	3 g salt
	5 g black pepper
For the beet chips	100 g beets (beetroots)
	300 ml vegetable oil
To serve	5 g fleur de sel
	6 g dill shoots

Turnips Using a mandolin, thinly slice the turnip. Put the sliced turnips in a medium skillet and cook over medium-low heat for 30 minutes, stirring occasionally, until the turnips release their moisture and then dry out and begin to stick to the bottom of the pan. Add the water, cover, and cook for 15 minutes over medium-low heat. Reduce the heat to low, stir in the yogurt, and cook for 5 minutes. Transfer the mixture to a Thermomix and mix on high speed at 175°F (80°C) for 10 minutes, or until smooth and homogeneous. Season with soy sauce.

White mussels Steam the mussels for between 30 seconds and 2 minutes, until the shells slightly open. Cool down immediately on a tray in an icy bain-marie. Open each mussel carefully.

Heat the brown butter (beurre noisette) in a skillet over low heat. Add the tucupi and bring to a boil. Whisk until emulsified.

Chiles Devein and seed the chiles, then cut into a brunoise. Put in a bowl, add the onion, olive oil, and vinegar, and mix. Season with salt and pepper.

Beet chips Using a mandolin, thinly slice the beets (beetroots) to a $1/16$-inch (1-mm) thickness. Heat a nonstick skillet over high heat. Add the beets to the pan and sear for 1 minute, turning frequently. Transfer the beets to a plate and pat dry with paper towel.

Heat the oil in a deep pan to 350°F (180°C). Carefully add the beets and fry for 2 minutes, turning frequently, until crispy. Transfer the beets to a plate lined with paper towel to drain. Pat dry. Keep in a dehydrator until needed.

To serve Bring the tucupi sauce to a boil over high heat. Add the mussels and warm for 30 seconds, or until they stew.

Spread the turnip puree on slightly deep plates. Top with mussels and tucupi sauce. Arrange 2 spoonfuls of chile mixture on the dish and another on top of the mussels. Place 3 beet chips on each plate, finishing with fleur de sel and dill shoots.

Leeks, cashew nuts, and vegetable sauce

I have a deep relationship with vegetables. They are a constant source of inspiration, and this dish represents my history and my connection to the countryside.

Serves 4

For the cashew nut paste
100 ml olive oil
40 g onion, brunoise
15 g garlic, brunoise
40 g tomato, seeded and chopped
5 g chile, seeded and chopped
70 ml Cashew Nut Oil (see page 142)
30 ml cumari pepper sauce
25 ml light soy sauce
13 ml lemon juice
5 g mint leaves
5 g salt

For the leeks
1 (8-inch/20-cm) leek stalk

For the vegetable sauce Part 1
3 kg carrots
1.26 kg tomatoes
190 g garlic head
300 g leek leaves (about 5)
50 ml light soy sauce
35 ml mirin
25 ml fish sauce (nam pla)
2 L water

Part 2
500 g leek stalks (about 5)
80 ml light soy sauce
50 ml rice vinegar
50 ml cranberry juice
50 g cold butter
50 g hydrated tapioca flour

For the wild rice crisp
200 ml sunflower oil
20 g wild rice
25 g Crispy Onion (see page 120)
5 g salt

For the green pasta
115 g spinach leaves
75 ml water
60 g egg
80 g all-purpose (plain) flour
0.5 g salt
semolina flour, for sprinkling

To serve
5 g brown butter (beurre noisette)
4 g fleur de sel, plus extra for finishing
1 quantity Cashew Nut Milk (see page 54)
4 g purple oxalis sprouts

Cashew nut paste
Heat the oil in a skillet over low heat. Add the onion and sauté for 10 minutes, until golden. Add the garlic and sauté for 1 minute, until fragrant. Add the tomatoes and chile and sauté for 20 minutes, until the mixture is dry. Stir in the cashew nut oil, cumari pepper sauce, soy sauce, and lemon juice and cook for 2 minutes. Transfer the mixture to a Thermomix and mix on high speed. Add the mint leaves and process until smooth. Season with salt, then pass the paste through a fine sieve. Set aside.

Leeks
Preheat a combination oven to 350°F (180°C) with 40% humidity. Add the leek and cook for 25 minutes, until tender. Remove the outer layers. Cut the leek into 2-inch (5-cm) pieces. Set aside.

Vegetable sauce Part 1
Cut the carrots into small pieces and run through a juicer. (Makes about 1.2 L.) Pour the juice into a saucepan and simmer over medium heat, until reduced by half. Set aside.

Preheat the oven to 350°F (180°C). Cut the tomatoes into 4 wedges and the garlic head in half. Cut the leek leaves into ¾ inch (2 cm) pieces. Place the vegetables in a roasting pan. Add the soy sauce, mirin, and fish sauce and stir to mix well. Bake for 1½ hours, stirring every 30 minutes, until golden brown. Pour in the water, scraping the bottom of the pan well to release the flavors. Bake for another 30 minutes. Remove the pan from the oven and strain the mixture through a chinois, squeezing well. Reserve the liquid.

Part 2
Preheat a charcoal barbecue over high heat. Roast the leeks directly on the hot coals, until slightly charred. Transfer to a cutting board and slice each stalk crosswise into 4 pieces.

In a saucepan, combine 1.5 liters roasted vegetable stock, 600 ml carrot reduction, soy sauce, vinegar, cranberry juice, and roasted leeks. Bring to a boil over medium heat and boil for 1 hour. Strain the mixture through a chinois, squeezing well. Return the strained mixture to the pan set over high heat and add the butter little by little, until slightly emulsified. Add the tapioca flour and mix until thickened.

Wild rice crisp
Heat the oil in a large skillet to 350°F (180°C). Add the wild rice and deep-fry until puffed up. Strain through a sieve, then transfer the wild rice to a plate lined with paper towel. In a bowl, combine the wild rice, crispy onion, and salt. Mix well, then spread out on paper towel.

Green pasta
Combine the spinach leaves and water in a saucepan. Bring to a boil over medium-high heat, then cover and stir for 5 minutes, or until the spinach is wilted and tender. Drain, then place the leaves in a bowl of ice water for 3 minutes. Drain the leaves again and squeeze well with your hands, extracting as much moisture as possible. Transfer the cooked spinach leaves to a blender, add the egg, and blend until smooth. Set aside.

Combine the flour and salt in a food processor and pulse to mix. Add the spinach mixture and pulse to form pea-size pieces. Sprinkle flour on a clean work surface and pour the mixture over top. Gather it together to create a dough and knead for 3 minutes, sprinkling in more semolina flour, if necessary, until firm and smooth. Wrap the dough in plastic wrap (clingfilm) and rest for 30 minutes.

Set a pasta maker to maximum thickness. Dust the work surface with semolina flour. Divide the dough into 2 portions. Wrap one portion in plastic wrap. Flatten the other portion and run it through the machine. Place the dough on the work surface and fold it in 3, as if it were a business letter. Sprinkle it with a little more semolina, then run it through the machine. Fold the dough and roll it 2 more times. Adjust the machine to the next thickness and roll again, repeating the folding process. Repeat until the dough is almost translucent. Cut into 6-inch (15-cm) squares. Sprinkle semolina in a bowl, then add the pasta squares, sprinkling more semolina between each layer to prevent them from sticking.

To serve
Bring a saucepan of salted water to a boil and cook the pasta for 10 seconds. Using a slotted spoon, transfer them to a plate. Spoon 1 teaspoon of cashew nut paste into the center of each plate. Heat the leek with the brown butter for 2 minutes. Arrange the leeks on the nut paste and season with fleur de sel. Drizzle cashew nut milk over the leek and pour over the vegetable sauce. Top the leek with the wild rice crisp. Lay a square of pasta on top. Finish with fleur de sel and oxalis.

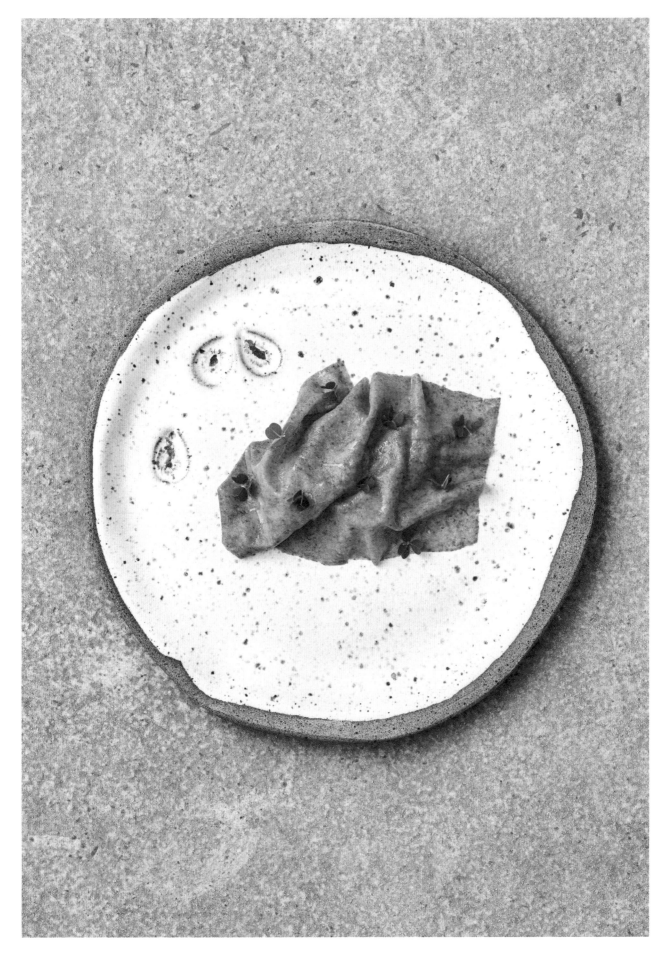

Sea bass, spicy lemon, and coconut sauce

This recipe began with lemon and coconut milk. I add lime and lemon to everything. One day I squeezed some lime over the milk and discovered it was a path we could explore even further. Once the herbs were added, the sauce was so good that we combined it with a quality white fish. The pumpkin seed oil completes the dish.

Serves 4

For the coconut milk	200 g fresh grated coconut 50 g powdered coconut milk 150 ml filtered water 50 ml fresh coconut water
For the pumpkin seed oil	500 g raw pumpkin seeds 500 ml sunflower oil 100 ml tucupi 1 cumari pepper
For the spicy lemon and coconut sauce	1 garlic clove 1 jalapeño 30 ml Pumpkin Seed Oil (see above) 60 g cilantro (coriander) 40 g sliced scallion (spring onion) 100 ml Coconut Milk (see above) 30 ml lemon juice salt, to season
For the sea bass	400 g sea bass 30 g brown butter (beurre noisette) 10 g sumac salt, to season

Coconut milk In a saucepan, combine the grated coconut, powdered coconut milk, and filtered water and boil for 10 minutes. Transfer to a Thermomix and mix for 6 minutes, then add the coconut water. In a clean dish towel (or new cloth diaper), strain the mixture into a bowl, squeezing well with your hands to extract all the milk.

Pumpkin seed oil Combine the pumpkin seeds and sunflower oil in a skillet over medium heat and cook for 18 minutes. Transfer the mixture to a Thermomix and mix for 8 minutes. Using a coffee filter, strain the mixture to separate the oil from the paste. In a bowl, combine 100 ml of oil, 50 g of paste, tucupi, and cumari pepper. Blend using an immersion blender.

Spicy lemon and coconut sauce Using a pestle and mortar, grind the garlic, jalapeño, and pumpkin seed oil until they form a fine paste. Add the cilantro (coriander) and sliced scallion (spring onion), then set aside for 10 minutes. Transfer to a bowl, add the coconut milk and lemon juice, and mix well. Season with salt.

Sea bass Preheat a combination oven to 212°F (100°C) with 100% humidity. Divide the fish into 4 x 100 g fillets and arrange on a baking sheet. Combine the brown butter (beurre noisette) and sumac in a small skillet over medium heat and stir until melted. Brush the fish with the mixture. Bake the fish for 3 minutes. Adjust the salt to taste.

To serve Arrange the sea bass on plates, spoon the spicy lemon and coconut sauce overtop, and finish with a drizzle of the pumpkin seed oil.

Octopus, black beans, and cashew nuts

I love eating salad with hot beans and vinegar or lime on top. This is often what I eat for lunch. One day I decided to combine beans with green apple to see if I could get closer to the taste I was seeking. It was not there yet, so I added some red apple puree. Then I created a sharp salsa with squid ink and cashew nuts. The octopus balances the recipe.

Serves 4

For the black beans Part 1	75 g black beans 150 ml cold water
Part 2	120 g red apple 60 g butter
Part 3	100 ml olive oil 20 g onion, brunoise 10 g garlic, brunoise 180 g green apple, brunoise 20 g pimenta de cheiro (green chile pepper) 20 g fresh yeast 12 g grated ginger 45 ml lime juice
For the crispy leeks	50 g leek leaves 200 ml sunflower oil
For the cashew nut sauce Part 1	30 g white miso paste 30 ml aged balsamic vinegar 15 ml sunflower oil 10 ml squid ink 5 ml cumari and tucupi sauce (such as the Manioca brand)
Part 2	100 g cashew nuts 40 g butter 30 g sliced scallion (spring onion) zest of 1 lime 5 g salt, to season
For the octopus	1 x 1.8 kg medium octopus 4 L water 330 g sliced onions 200 g bacon 100 g garlic 100 g Italian parsley
To serve	20 g brown butter (beurre noisette)

For the black beans Part 1 In a large bowl, soak the black beans in the cold water for 24 hours.

Part 2 Core the unpeeled apple. Using a mandolin, thinly slice it. Melt the butter in a skillet over medium heat. Add the apple and braise for 18 minutes, or until it becomes a creamy puree.

Part 3 Heat the oil in a Dutch oven (casserole) over medium heat. Add the onion and braise for 12 minutes, or until withered. Add the garlic and braise for another 5 minutes. Add 180 g hydrated black beans and their soaking water, green apple, chile, yeast, and ginger. Bring to a boil and boil for 30 minutes, or until the beans are tender. Put the beans and lime juice in a Thermomix and mix on high speed. Add 100 g apple puree to correct the acidity and mix on high speed again. Transfer to a sieve and, while hot, strain into a bowl. Set aside.

Crispy leeks Cut the leek leaves into 3¼-inch (8-cm) strips. Put them in a skillet along with the olive oil. Cook over medium heat, moving all the time, keeping the heat always under 350°F (180°C). Transfer the leeks to a plate lined with paper towel to drain, then place in a dehydrator for 8 hours to crisp.

Cashew nut sauce Part 1 In a bowl, whisk together all the ingredients.

Part 2 Coarsely chop the cashews. In a skillet, combine the butter and cashews over medium heat and sauté for 8 minutes, or until browned. Remove the skillet from the heat, then add the scallion (spring onion) and lime zest. Season with salt. Add the sauce from part 1 to the seasoned cashews and stir to mix. Set aside.

Octopus Clean the octopus, remove its head and beak, and set aside. Combine the water, onions, bacon, garlic, and parsley in a stockpot and bring to a boil. Using steel tongs, carefully dunk the octopus into the boiling water. Quickly repeat this dunking action 12 times to maintain the octopus skin during the cooking process, then lower the octopus into the stockpot and cook for 30–50 minutes at 267°F (130°C), until soft and tender. Transfer the octopus to a large bowl of ice water for 15 minutes, or until it becomes really cold. Transfer the octopus to a cutting board and slice its tentacles into 4-inch (10-cm) lengths.

To serve Combine the brown butter (beurre noisette) and octopus in a skillet over high heat and cook for about 3 minutes on each side, until crispy.

Heat the bean puree in a small pot over low heat. Spread hot bean puree on each plate. Top with a spoonful of cashew nut sauce and arrange the golden octopus overtop. Finish with crispy leeks.

Lamb, onions, and peanuts

This recipe was built around peanuts. We had a lot of them, and I hate wasting food. So I created a seasoned peanut butter to combine with the lamb rack. I buy lamb from a farmer I trust deeply, so I can serve it pink (page 111). The rest of the ingredients followed, to balance the flavors.

Serves 4

For the cashew and nori paste	2 g ground cumin
	2 g pink peppercorns
	2 (7- × 8-inch/18- × 20-cm) toasted nori sheets
	100 ml Coconut Milk (see page 68)
	75 ml Cashew Nut Oil (see page 142)
	20 ml rice vinegar
For the onion puree	500 g white onions
	17 ml rice vinegar
	35 ml Cashew Nut Oil (see page 142)
	5 g hydrated tapioca flour
	salt, to season
Honey vinaigrette	30 ml emerina native bee honey
	10 ml olive oil
	2 g salt
	2 g black pepper
For the mustard leaves	10 ml emerina native bee honey
	10 ml rice vinegar
	salt, to season
	black pepper, to season
	2 mustard leaves
	500 ml water
For the peanut butter	3 ml olive oil
	50 g peanuts
	6 g red onion, brunoise
	10 g garlic, brunoise
	8 g tomato, brunoise
	6 g malagueta pepper, brunoise
	8 ml light soy sauce
	1 makrut lime leaf
	4 g sliced cilantro (coriander)
	4 g chopped Italian parsley
	0.5 g hot paprika
	0.2 g ground cinnamon
For the lamb rack	2 g fine pink salt
	2 g sugar
	1 x 500 g lamb rack
	olive oil, to season
	salt, to season
	black pepper, to season
	50 g brown butter (beurre noisette)
	50 g cubed cold butter
	5 g fleur de sel
To serve	80g ml Demi-Glace (see page 160)

Cashew and nori paste   In a small blender, blend the cumin and pink peppercorns to a fine powder. Place the nori in a blender and blend to a powder. Add the cumin-peppercorn powder and coconut milk and blend for 5 minutes. Add the cashew nut oil and vinegar and blend on high speed for another 5 minutes, or until the mixture is smooth. Set aside.

Onion puree   Preheat the oven to 347°F (175°C).

Bake the whole onions, unpeeled, for 1 hour, until soft and caramelized. Remove from the oven, peel, and cut into quarters. Cook the quartered onions in a heavy-bottomed skillet over medium heat for 30 minutes, or until they dry, become more caramelized, and stick slightly to the bottom of the pan. Add the vinegar and cook until the liquid has evaporated.

Transfer the onions to a Thermomix and mix on high speed at 175°F (80°C) for 10 minutes, or until soft and homogenous. Add the cashew nut oil and mix for 5 minutes on high speed at 175°F (80°C). With the motor running, add the hydrated tapioca flour little by little, until it binds. Season with salt and set aside.

Honey vinaigrette   Using an immersion blender, blend all the ingredients until emulsified.

Mustard leaves   In a bowl, combine the honey and vinegar. Season with salt and pepper.

Cut the mustard leaves in half.

Bring the water to a boil in a saucepan. Prepare a bowl with ice water. Add the mustard leaves to the saucepan and blanch for 3 seconds. Transfer them to a bowl with ice water. Remove the leaves and pat dry with paper towel.

Peanut butter   Heat the olive oil in a heavy-bottomed skillet over medium-low heat. Add the peanuts and toast for 10 minutes. Add the onion and sauté for 12 minutes, or until browned. Stir in the garlic and sauté for another 20 minutes, or until browned.

Add the tomato, malagueta pepper, soy sauce, and lime leaf and sauté for 10 minutes, or until dry. Add the cilantro (coriander), parsley, hot paprika, and cinnamon and sauté until fragrant. Transfer the mixture to a blender and blend until creamy and homogenous. Set aside.

Lamb rack   Combine the salt and the sugar, then sprinkle the mixture all over the lamb. Place on a wire rack over a baking sheet and refrigerate, uncovered, for 8 hours to cure. Remove the lamb from the refrigerator and pat dry with paper towel.

Preheat a combination oven to 350°F (180°C) with 30% humidity.

Cut the meat into 4 equal portions. Season with olive oil, salt, and pepper. Heat a skillet over high heat, then add the brown butter (beurre noisette) and lamb racks. Sear each side for 20 seconds. Add the cubed butter and baste the lamb for 30 seconds.

Transfer the lamb to a roasting pan and baste with the butter from the skillet. Place the lamb in the oven for 3 minutes. Transfer the lamb to a wire rack and let rest for 5 minutes. Pour any leftover pan butter into a small saucepan and keep it warm. After 5 minutes, baste the lamb with this butter and season with fleur de sel.

To serve   Spread a spoonful of onion puree on each plate. Place a lamb rack to one side and drizzle with demi-glace. Brush the mustard leaves with the honey vinaigrette and toast them with a kitchen torch. Use each leaf to cover part of the lamb. Add a spoonful of peanut butter to the plate and top the mustard leaves with a small spoonful of cashew and nori paste. Serve immediately.

Carrot, leaven, and cassava

Vegetables are an essential part of a Manu menu. We want to reflect the best version of them and always respect their freshness and the farm they come from. I have always wanted a carrot recipe, and I am proud that this is one of my most memorable dishes (page 111).

There are three key things about this recipe: The first is to harvest the carrots during a crescent moon, when they are at their sweetest. The second is to leave them unpeeled and wash them carefully. The third is to steam them for 8–12 minutes (depending on size), so that the carrots retain their structure. If in doubt, steam for 8 minutes.

Serves 4

For the rub
50 ml olive oil
25 g cumin seeds
18 g garlic, crushed
14 g brown sugar
3 g pink peppercorns

For the carrots
8 carrots with 4½ inches (12 cm) of tops

For the leaven dressing
140 g fresh sourdough starter
120 ml light soy sauce
120 ml water
50 ml rice vinegar
8 g garlic
100 g cubed cold butter

For the crumb
25 g butter
60 g onion, brunoise
100 g cassava flour, such as Bragança flour
zest of 2 lemons
15 g chopped Italian parsley
15 g chopped cilantro (coriander)
salt, to season

Rub — Put all the ingredients in a food processor and blend.

Carrots — Wash the carrots. Keep them unpeeled and steam for 8–12 minutes, until tender. While they are still hot, lightly toss them with the rub. Set aside to cool.

Leaven dressing — In a blender, blend the sourdough starter, soy sauce, water, vinegar, and garlic until smooth. Transfer the dressing to a saucepan and warm over medium heat. Add the cubed butter, stirring with a whisk until emulsified.

Crumb — Heat the butter in a Dutch oven (casserole) over low heat for 10 minutes, or until browned. Add the onion and sauté for 10 minutes, or until browned. Add the cassava flour and stir for about 6 minutes, until crispy.

Remove from the heat. Add the lemon zest, parsley, and cilantro (coriander). Season with salt.

To serve — Preheat a grill to high (500°F/260°C). Grill the carrots for 2 minutes on each side, until browned. Put 2 hot carrots on each plate. Pour the leaven dressing overtop and finish with the crumb.

Kiwi and yerba mate béarnaise

Paraná is the largest producer of yerba mate, producing more than eighty percent of the yerba consumed in Brazil. South Brazilians drink yerba mate every day, and we customarily chat over a cup of yerba mate rather than a cup of coffee. A meal with a yerba mate dessert connects me to family and acquaintances, and just thinking of that makes my heart melt.

Serves 4

For the lemon cream	5 lemons
	80 g butter
	200 g sugar
	200 ml heavy (double) cream
For the dehydrated kiwi	3 kiwis
For the kiwi sorbet	455 g sliced and frozen kiwis
	85 ml jataí native bee honey
For the yerba mate béarnaise	75 g yerba mate powder
	100 ml rice vinegar
	100 ml white wine
	50 g sugar
	250 g butter
	45 g egg yolks

Lemon cream Cut the lemons in half. Melt the butter in a skillet over medium heat. Add the lemons, flesh side down, and cook for 8 minutes. Transfer the lemons to a glass container with a lid and add the sugar. Set aside at room temperature for 7 days to ferment.

Put the cream in a large bowl. Whisk in the juice from the fermented lemon preparation little by little (30 ml at a time). Transfer to a container and refrigerate until needed.

Dehydrated kiwi Thinly slice the unpeeled kiwis, then place them in a dehydrator for 10 hours at 108°F (42°C). Reserve.

Kiwi sorbet Put the kiwis and honey in a pacotizing beaker and process. Freeze for 6 hours. Mix in the pacotizing beaker before serving.

Yerba mate béarnaise In a saucepan, combine 50 g of yerba mate powder, vinegar, white wine, and sugar and cook over low heat for 30 minutes, or until reduced by three-quarters. Strain.

Combine the butter and the remaining 25 g of yerba mate powder in a skillet and heat over low heat for 20 minutes, or until foamy. Strain.

Place the egg yolks in a bowl, then heat over low heat in a water bath. Whisk in the yerba mate reduction until emulsified and aerated. Whisk in the yerba mate butter until creamy.

To serve Spread some yerba mate béarnaise on each plate. Top with lemon cream, then a quenelle of kiwi sorbet. Finish with the dehydrated kiwi.

Tucupi, coconut, and peanuts

I have fond memories of my grandmother's coconut cake. I revisited this recipe for a dessert at the restaurant. In the original version, she used condensed milk to moisten the cake, but at the restaurant we use a peanut milk. And we serve it with yogurt ice cream. The punch comes from the tucupi salsa, which no one else in Brazil dares to use in a dessert.

Serves 4

For the peanut milk	150 g roasted peanuts
	500 ml water
	25 g sugar
For the yogurt ice cream	500 g plain (natural) yogurt
	120 g quark cheese
	100 g confectioners' (icing) sugar
	80 ml whole (full-fat) milk
	50 ml heavy (double) cream
For the tucupi salsa	1 L tucupi
	100 g cilantro (coriander)
	100 g micro basil leaves
	100 ml passion fruit juice
	50 ml sour passion fruit juice
	60 g tapioca pearls
For the coconut cake	100 ml whole (full-fat) milk
	60 ml Coconut Milk (see page 68)
	90 g eggs
	120 g all-purpose (plain) flour
	60 g room-temperature butter
	100 g sugar
	12 g baking powder
For the coconut bacon	30 g brown sugar
	35 ml light soy sauce
	7.5 ml liquid smoke
	16 coconut ribbons (about 60 g)
	00 g butter
To serve	6 g cilantro (coriander) leaves (optional)

Peanut milk Hydrate the peanuts in 300 ml of water for 24 hours. Drain the water, then transfer the peanuts to a Thermomix and add the remaining 200 ml of water and sugar. Mix on high speed for 15 minutes at 194°F (90°C). Set aside to cool.

Yogurt ice cream Combine all the ingredients in a pacotizing beaker. Seal the beaker and freeze at −8°F (−22°C) for at least 24 hours. Mix 2 hours before use.

Tucupi salsa Heat the tucupi in a saucepan over medium heat until warmed through. Remove from the heat, then stir in the cilantro (coriander) and basil. Cover and set aside for 2 hours to infuse the flavors. Strain the tucupi into another saucepan, add the passion fruit juices and simmer over low heat, until the liquid has reduced to 400 ml. Stir in the tapioca pearls and whisk until the stock has thickened. Strain the mixture into another saucepan and let cool.

Heat the mixture over medium heat for 5–10 minutes to thicken. Using an immersion blender, blend the mixture until smooth. Refrigerate until needed.

Coconut cake Preheat the oven to 350°F (180°C). In a bowl, whisk together the milk, coconut milk, and eggs.

In another bowl, sift the flour.

In the bowl of a stand mixer fitted with the paddle attachment, beat the butter and sugar on medium speed until doubled in volume. Reduce the speed and slowly incorporate the wet ingredients and the flour, alternating them. Add the baking powder and gently mix until fully incorporated.

Pour the batter into a greased baking pan and bake for 25–30 minutes. Set aside to cool, then cut into 5/8-inch (1.5-cm) squares. Transfer the cake to a bowl and soak in the peanut milk to moisten. Refrigerate until needed.

Coconut bacon In a mixing bowl, combine the brown sugar, soy sauce, and liquid smoke and mix until the sugar has dissolved. Add the coconut ribbons and marinate for 30 minutes. Drain the ribbons.

Melt the butter in a nonstick skillet over medium heat. Add the coconut ribbons and fry for 10 minutes, turning frequently, until completed dried out and crispy. Transfer to a plate lined with paper towel to cool. Keep the coconut ribbons in a dehydrator until needed.

To serve Put 25 ml of tucupi salsa in each bowl. Add a spoonful of moistened cake and top with a quenelle of yogurt ice cream. Place 2 slices of coconut bacon on top and finish with the cilantro (coriander) leaves, if using. Serve immediately.

Popsicle 2.0

This dessert, our second popsicle, revolutionized the menu at Manu. The first (1.0) was made with Brazil nut milk (page 168). In the second version (2.0), we better understood how to make it, and we used cheap little South American peanuts.

The peanuts in this popsicle are special. They are produced by Divonci Mariano from Vale e Cia, who also supplies the brown sugar and the molasses used at the restaurant (page 104). We receive the peanuts raw in the bean and with plenty of dirt, so we allow a generous amount of time for making the milk.

The recipe also uses a coffee from Terezinha das Graças Rodrigues at Distinto Café, a producer from the city of Pinhalão (page 106) who passed away recently. I had a strong connection with her. I am touched by the metamorphosis that we, the cooks at Manu, make with these extraordinary ingredients from these remarkable farmers.

Serves 4

For the peanut milk	300 g raw peanuts 450 ml whole (full-fat) milk
For the peanut popsicle	90 g egg yolks (about 5) 100 g sugar 300 ml heavy (double) cream 300 ml Peanut Milk (see above) fleur de sel, for sprinkling
To serve	coffee bean shavings, for sprinkling

Peanut milk Heat a heavy-bottomed skillet over high heat. Add the peanuts and toast for 15 minutes, stirring continuously to prevent them from burning.

Transfer the peanuts to a blender, add the milk, and blend on high speed for 10 minutes. Strain the milk through a chinois or cheesecloth (muslin). Set aside.

Peanut popsicle In the bowl of a stand mixer fitted with the whisk attachment, beat the egg yolks and sugar until pale.

Combine the cream and peanut milk in a small saucepan and warm slightly. Pour the mixture little by little into the stand mixer, gently mixing until fully incorporated.

Transfer the mixture to a bain marie and cook for about 10 minutes, never allowing it to exceed 140°F (60°C). Set aside to cool completely. Pour the mixture into silicone popsicle molds and sprinkle fleur de sel over the top of each. Freeze for at least 6 hours, until frozen.

To serve Remove the popsicles from the molds and place on a tray of ice. Sprinkle with the coffee bean shavings and serve immediately.

Melon and pork

My maternal grandmother comes from an Italian family, and many of her dinner parties start with Parma ham and cantaloupe. I was inspired to create a dessert using that flavor combination. My eldest daughter, Helena, loves using cassava flour to add crunch to ice cream, and it also goes well with the melon ice cream, and the lard, in this dish. In this recipe, three generations of my family are reflected on the same plate.

Serves 4

For the melon ice cream	300 g sour cream
	130 g sugar
	500 g peeled cantaloupe, brunoise
	5 ml lime juice
For the crumbs	25 g lard
	15 g butter
	75 g raw flaked cassava flour
	1 g fleur de sel
For the pork fat	1 g dried juniper
	1 g pink peppercorns
	1 g grated amburana
	100 g bacon fat, chopped into small cubes
To serve	5 g fleur de sel
	3 g cilantro (coriander) leaves

Melon Ice cream Combine the sour cream and sugar in a saucepan and bring to a boil over medium heat. Transfer to a blender and set aside until cooled to 122°F (50°C).

Add the melon and lime juice to the blender and blend well. Strain the mixture through a chinois into a freezer-proof container. Chill at 39°F (4°C) for at least 12 hours. Put the mixture into an ice-cream machine and churn, following the manufacturer's directions. Keep the ice cream at 28°F (−2°C) until needed.

Crumbs Preheat the oven to 275°F (135°C).

Melt the lard and butter in a skillet over 284°F (140°C) heat. Remove the skillet from the heat and stir in the flaked cassava flour for 7 minutes, or until crunchy. Spread the mixture on a baking sheet and bake for 25 minutes, stirring the mixture occasionally. Remove from the oven and let cool. Season with fleur de sel.

Pork fat Using a pestle and mortar, combine the juniper and pink peppercorns and grind well. Stir in the grated amburana.

Heat a heavy-bottomed skillet over medium heat. Add the bacon and sauté for 8 minutes. Reduce the heat to medium-low and sauté until rendered and the bacon becomes crunchy. Strain the fat through a chinois into a bowl. Add the spice blend, mixing well.

To serve Put a spoonful of crumbs into each bowl. Place a quenelle of melon ice cream on the crumbs. Drizzle pork fat all around. Finish with a pinch of fleur de sel and cilantro (coriander) leaves overtop the ice cream.

Melipona

This genus of stingless bees is found throughout the southern hemisphere, except for in Antarctica. They improve their surrounding environments by pollinating the nearby plants and improving the quality of the crops. Social ties are crucial to the organization, and success, of the colonies.

Aloisio Selhorst's unique, handcrafted knives are made with carbon-steel laminate and noble wooden handles.

Mistakes, faith, and adulthood

It was never about luck. It was always about hard work. Yes, I come from a good family. That helped a lot, but nothing in my life came easily to me. For every penny I got from my dad, I had to answer one question: "What are you going to do better to deserve it?" Both my father and mother worked hard their entire lives, and I modeled their work ethic. I do not have enough fingers on my hands to count the days I labored while friends, family, and acquaintances were partying and having fun.

There were indeed mistakes. To become what I am today, I failed... a lot.

When I opened Manu, few restaurants in Brazil at the time did tasting menus exclusively, as I've been doing since day one. Alex Atala in São Paulo and Claude Troisgros in Rio de Janeiro had both à la carte and tasting menus. During Saturday lunches at my grandparents' home, I'd frequently be asked, "Aren't you going to serve risotto and steak? Everybody loves it." No, I was not going to have it on Manu's menu. Fine dining was my cup of tea.

I wanted to offer my guests an experience. I wanted to invite them to leave their comfort zone: to experience traditional flavors in different "outfits" and be surprised by unusual textures and combinations. Unfortunately, I had few management skills, and I rarely limited my ingredient budgets—I simply wanted all the finest ingredients all the time. I knew that fresh and seasonal ingredients were best, but I also believed fine dining was about Wagyu beef and white linen tablecloths. I try not to think about the money I spent on laundry or the number of times I was disappointed to see wrinkled tablecloths, incorrectly folded napkins, and uneven table dressing trims. I would often take Manu's laundry to my mother's, to make sure it was done my way.

But the real extravagances were with the shopping lists. I wanted only the most expensive and most exotic ingredients—I thought my talent would be most evident if I demonstrated how well I could prepare Kobe steak, colossal shrimp (tiger prawns), and lobsters. The flowers on the table were, of course, the most exquisite I could afford. I didn't yet realize that my trusted team of produce, fish, and meat suppliers (all of whom I've worked with since the first day of the restaurant) and my culinary skills would be enough to create my brand and the "emotional" kitchen I stand for. The sets that my team and I create today, with the flowers and foliage cut from the restaurant's nearby trees and shrubs, express Manu's essence more effectively than expensive tulips and orchids ever did.

And then there were the knives. Today, it amuses me to see new chefs armed with high-carbon German steel knives, Japanese chopping knives, Swiss broad-blade knives, or any other marketed knife style. But I was there once, too. A drawer full of them never seemed enough, even though I wield them in one hand only. I missed several celebratory moments at home by accepting invitations from chefs to journey to some distant knife store in order to add another "must-have" blade to my arsenal.

With time I came to understand the city's rhythm—and this meant coping with summer lulls when customers were out of town on vacation, and many Mondays and Tuesdays without diners. I also learned to understand my clients, finding ways to surprise them, such as peppering the restaurant's playlist with Brazilian music.

In 2013, I opened the brasserie MB on the same street as Manu to showcase simpler dishes in a more relaxed atmosphere. I rented the entire floor of a commercial building and had a huge personal office, a massive team, and fancy changing rooms for employees. What a mistake! From this experience, I learned that some people are unscrupulous, debts can accumulate rapidly, and a restaurant must be self-sufficient. And that I enjoy the creation of original dishes. The time devoted to producing each ingredient is precious, and I appreciate the development of their flavors before creating my recipes with them.

By January 2014, my nights were ending with a bottle of wine. And on numerous Sundays, my husband would need to assure me that I was an able cook. I had little money for my expenses, and I was too proud to ask for help. I put on a lot of weight and slept poorly. In March of that year, I discovered that I was pregnant with my first daughter, Helena. One day, my husband and I went to the seaside, where I told him I wanted to quit. I'd had enough with cooking; I would grow cassava and corn on my father's farm, take care of the sheep, and live the peaceful life of my childhood. I cry easily, and I was in tears when Dario stopped the car to calm me down.

I am very religious. In my field, you rarely find chefs admitting to this. On my worst days, I visited the sanctuary of Our Lady of Aparecida, Brazil's patron saint, and to whom I feel a strong connection. After a 360-mile (580-kilometer) drive from Curitiba to Aparecida, Dario and I arrived at the world's second-largest basilica, where up to 30,000 people can fill the pews. In a small chapel within the cathedral, a priest preached his sermon to congregants. Matthew 6:33–34, to be precise: "But seek first His kingdom and the righteousness, and all these things will be given to you as well. Therefore do not worry about tomorrow, for tomorrow will worry about itself. Each day has enough trouble of its own." These verses were, for me, a bridge over troubled waters. I decided to solve each problem, one by one. I closed the bistro so I could commit to my focus on my family, Manu, and my career, in that order.

My first daughter was born the following January, and I started down a new path. The pain of coming to maturity was over. Failure is part of the process. And it will happen over and over again. I had to overcome obstacles to find clarity in my goals and purpose. I knew I was strong enough to pursue the dream of being the best chef I could be.

Welcome drink and pairing

When conducting research for Manu, I spent a great deal of time looking into good kitchen utensils, the best stove, heat-resistant kitchen tiles, and durable floor ceramics. But I also went back to my maternal grandmother's book. She comes from a time when chefs believed recipes were their superpowers and should be kept under lock and key. Her recipes could be found in books for homemakers. I can still conjure up the smell of the yellowed pages—all 500 of them—of her 1960s cookbook *A arte de receber amigos* (meaning "the art of receiving friends"). In it you could find the recipe for fermented pineapple juice that my grandmother served as an aperitif at her parties. The recipe was simple: wash the pineapple, cut the fruit into small cubes, and do the same with the peels. Combine everything in a large jar and fill it with water. Cover and set aside for three days. To serve, stir the liquid and squeeze the peels well to extract the flavor. Add sugar, if necessary, and serve cold.

I had an idea for a welcome drink to start the menu. Fermentation is an integral part of our preparations at Manu. I ferment milk, mushrooms, and vegetables. I like the umami of these preparations, which connects with an area in the center of the tongue, close to the throat. To open the meal with a fermented non-alcoholic drink is to provide a window onto what is to come in Manu's tasting menu. My team loves brainstorming about this drink. We've made it with pineapple, chayote and salt, sweet potatoes, coffee, and even fermented grapes—an old family recipe that has fresh grape juice sitting overnight at room temperature.

In some ways, this welcome drink inspired our pairings at the restaurant. We have offered this service since opening, and I genuinely believe that a good pairing elevates the diner's experience. I am lucky to count on Juli Rodrigues, the sommelier who has worked with me since 2014. She understands my work and how I create dishes. She always says that, when it comes to the pairing for Manu, it is necessary to eat all of the dish, since I work with nuances that unfold up to the last bite. After she tries the dish, we discuss which aspect we will build on in the beverage pairing. For spicy dishes, we like to find a wine with some sweetness. If the dish has animal fat or lots of cream or butter, we will lean toward more acidic wines to attenuate and honor the greasiness. I have learned a tremendous amount from her, and I give her space to trust her instincts. The wine world is virtually infinite—it is crucial that I have someone by my side who can complement the food.

At the moment, half the wines we pair with Manu's dishes are Brazilian. We are lucky to be near the best national producers and try to visit them at least four times a year. I believe in the potential of Brazilian wines, especially whites and rosés. Most of the wines we serve are natural and biodynamic, use zero or minimal sulfites, and have no additives. We look for small winemakers who produce wines in limited batches and with minimal intervention, using traditional techniques, unadulterated fermented grapes, and native yeast. We meet them at fairs, through visits to vineyards, and via referrals—the search is ongoing. Our list is long, and we change the wine offerings constantly to make room for as many producers as possible. We prefer unfiltered wines and love to know about the character of the grapes, the condition of production, how they decided on the wine's name, and even what was considered when making the product's label. Any interesting story about the bottle will be relayed to customers during the pairing. Every bottle opened at the restaurant comes from a sustainable farm whose owners care for the land and the people who work on it. As soon as I tried natural wines in Europe, I understood that these types of wine aligned with my concepts, and I began the search for quality Brazilian wines to serve at the restaurant. (In fact, I was one of the first chefs in Brazil to work with natural wines.) Even though wine is often the best pairing option, we also look at beers and sakes.

From time to time, happy surprises arise during our exchanges with suppliers, such as learning about the Projeto Seiva infusions, made with grapes harvested at the same farm where Vinha Unna wines are produced, in southern Brazil. The farm researched the techniques of making traditional *Camellia sinensis* tea, adapted it to the biodynamic calendar, and started cultivating native herbs from forests in southern Brazil. The infusions are delicate yet rich in flavor and perfect for those who prefer not to drink coffee at the end of our menu.

Instead of sodas, we offer homemade kombucha, thanks to a good supplier that provides different flavors of this fermented drink. We also have freshly squeezed Brazilian fruit juices, such as taperebá, cupuaçu, and bacuri. These fruits are so naturally sweet that we don't add sugar. As well, we offer a drink called *tudo são flores* (which translates as "It's all about flowers"), which is made with hidraflor, a wild fermented beverage prepared by a small family who harvests the fresh flowers used in it according to the moon phases. They believe the phases of the moon add medicinal properties to the flowers and want to explore it in the drink. Each month, they send a different drink made with flowers specific to that month. I am a fan of their philosophy and their delicate and beautiful drinks, which complement our in-house hibiscus fermentation.

I strongly believe in being the change I want to see. I feel fortunate to be a cook and to meet such a diverse and exciting group of like-minded people who want to enact change through food and drink. As time goes on, I see the Manu family growing and the reality of making good choices daily. We are already a large community, and I will always find quality products to help each detail of Manu's restaurant menu be special, seasonal, and unique. I hope our example will prove that this change is possible.

Table configuration, routine, and evolution

My kitchen is uncomplicated. I have the basics (good knife, precision straight tongs, saucier spoon, good pans, and so on), a hand mixer, and a stand mixer. All my ice creams can be hand-shaken. My food is about mixing unimagined flavors and textures, like cauliflower and passion fruit. It requires technique, precision, and attention to the cook point of each ingredient.

I believe that our taste buds change every day. Every time I go to the market or travel, I discover a new flavor and add something to my library of tastes. When I cook, I am immersed in creating the best dish. And every night, I carry out the same exercise several times. After I try something I've prepared, I close my eyes and wait for the missing flavor to appear to me. I love these moments. When I designed Manu, I wanted it to be a food destination that reflected my soul. I scrutinized every detail of the restaurant, from the furniture to the choice of flooring to the exterior and interior doors. I transported a lot of sand in the trunk (boot) of my car to build the new walls.

I wanted to create a space where patrons could leave their problems, politics, and family issues at the door. The color palette and the composition of the dining room were designed to invite the diner to notice the subtleties of every bite and the enjoyment of celebrating food at a dinner table. The restaurant has had various table configurations over the years, but it now has five four-top tables (that can quickly become two- or five-top tables) in a large open hall overlooking the open kitchen to one side. On the other side is a big window facing the street.

Our first reservation is for 6 p.m., and whoever arrives has to ring the doorbell, as if they are arriving at my home. They are welcomed with a smile by a front-of-house staff member and guided to their table, where a welcome drink is served. Then the journey of flavors begins with the explanation of the menu, which always features seasonal, hyperlocal, and sustainable ingredients.

To make all this possible, the routine starts at 8 a.m., when Bruno Cabral arrives. He handles the prep work, prepares the mise en place, and receives all the deliveries—fish from Trapiche Pescados on Wednesday; the shellfish and other fish from Inácio Pescados on Thursday and Friday; and all the fresh and organic produce every Wednesday and Friday. Anyone else who arrives early helps with the sourdough. At 10:30 a.m., Henrique Lorkievicz, the poissonier, arrives. At noon, sous-chefs Debora Teixeira and Lucas Correia arrive. Carlos Eduardo Chaves, or Carlitos, my steward and the oldest—and calmest—member (now in his fifties) of my long-time team, arrives at noon. He cleans the dishes and cookware, and organizes the storeroom. At 1 p.m., the dining-room staff—Juli Rodrigues, Deibd Rodrigues, Emiliano Lauriano, Jean Santana—and Vanessa, the pastry chef, arrive. We have an intern who works from 9 a.m. to 3 p.m. And a second one who comes at 4 p.m. and leaves at 10 p.m. I sometimes arrive very early to have the kitchen to myself. But usually I'm at the restaurant at 2 p.m., after my driver Nivaldo dos Santos and I do the daily shopping. He has been with me for ages and knows me well enough to even shop on my behalf for ingredients.

Our menu starts with homemade bread and features nine to ten dishes, two desserts, and petit fours. We also present a food gift (page 95) for guests to take home and enjoy the following day. My idea is for them to make a connection with the previous night and recall good times. We do not work with station chefs at Manu but with plate divisions. Each chef is responsible for arranging three to four dishes each night.

I take good care of how my menus are designed and printed. I spend a lot of time looking for the best paper, which must be recycled, sustainable, and have a good feel to the touch. I buy papers at a particular store near my house. The one I like most is made with banana and onion skin, so delicate and warm at the same time. I also take time to consider the dish names, the menu titles, and the introductory words for each tasting menu.

My recent menu, Metamorphosis (page 53), is about evolution. About maturing and soaring. About changing forms, structures, and nature. We are not the same person we were a month or even a minute ago. Life is in constant motion, with growth and experience. Food is always around us. The Metamorphosis menu is finished with a carrot instead of meat, which tradition has always dictated. It's a testament to how my work has evolved and how I always seek change in my kitchen.

Strength, connections, and notebooks

New staff members and interns at Manu must perform this exercise: sit in the dining room and watch the kitchen. First we ask them to observe the kitchen when it is empty, and then again when we are preparing food. Manu's open kitchen is white—it is the food and staff who introduce color and warmth to the space—like a blank sheet on which a story will be printed each night. This simple exercise of observation is immensely useful. Employees report that it helped them fall readily into the restaurant's routine. They understand my obsession with a clean and tidy kitchen and the need for quiet concentration while working. Our guests can see us and feel the mood, and they know we are there to create a pleasurable and enjoyable experience.

My stages in Piedmont with *la famiglia Cerea* at Da Vittorio and with Guido Alciati and Lidia Vanzino at Guido Restaurant had a massive impact on my cooking philosophy and approach to running a restaurant. These restaurateurs rely on tradition, heirloom family recipes, cutting-edge techniques, and attentive hospitality. The space should be warm and bright—somewhere you want to stay for the duration of a meal. During the two seasons I staged at Noma, I took a careful look at the community and considered each ingredient, where it came from, and who was behind it. René and his team were passionate about Scandinavia and sought out all ingredients the land offered. After my time with the Noma team, I had a new perspective of my own country and had acquired a newfound pride in Brazil and its land.

In the months leading up to the opening of Manu, I was engrossed in my notebooks—scribbling down notes, drawing conclusions of what I wanted (or didn't want), and creating loads of to-do lists (I was fond of the stationery!). While I am very connected on social media, I cannot resist the touch of paper, and notebooks especially. Since I was an adolescent, I've written everything down in notebooks. In my home office, two desk drawers are packed with more than fifty notebooks dating from the past twenty years. I went back to them when I was imagining my restaurant space. Some of the notebooks are spiral-bound; others more traditionally bound. Some have hard covers; others, soft. They vary in size and color as well. One notebook in particular stands out. Purchased in 2003, just before my trip to Europe, with Paris as my first stop, this 200-page notebook features on its cover the image of a vintage postcard of the Arc de Triomphe and the silhouette of a woman wearing a slinky cocktail dress and black top hat. In it are diary entries and mementos from the trip—itineraries and lists of destinations, including museums, I wanted to visit—plus notes from the first hospitality courses I completed a few years later in Curitiba.

My recent notebooks have either kraft-paper or black hardboard covers. I cannot survive without my notebooks, and I expect my team to take notes of my instructions, because I record everything I ask of them. Patience is not among my virtues. I prefer doing over waiting.

Upon reflection, looking back at my notes, I can see my path developing and taking shape. I've always been attached to people and celebrations, and when I started culinary school, recipes didn't concern me. Pages were decorated with notes about ingredient characteristics, best methods for their preparations, and optimal harvesting seasons. As for my restaurant-to-be, I wanted a celebratory place that looked like my house, where we would serve unbelievably good and provocative food that provided guests with a sensorial experience. I wanted to offer patrons a new perspective on food.

Part of my research involved listening attentively to my grandparents' stories. With them, I revisited both our celebratory and everyday meals. These included Claudete's crunchy bruschetta with fresh spinach or corn cream, served at our Maringá home, or her unforgettable banana cake made with two types of banana and oat flour—she ground whole oats a dozen times until it was transformed into fine flour for the cake. That recipe is so important to me that I've recreated it as a gift for Manu guests to take home.

At the restaurant, our brown sugar, butter, cream, nut milks, and some flours are homemade. To this day, insiders know where to find the little black mark on the inside corner of Manu's back door, caused from cracking open Brazil nuts. (Until I sourced a good supplier of shelled Brazil nuts, we had to open the nuts by closing the back door on them.) I went to a little farm next to my house to buy the milk of Odara the cow. This free-roaming cow happily grazes in a green field, eating well. We use very little dairy at Manu, but the yogurt, butter, and milk we do use come from the milk of this happy cow.

It is nice to sit at a Manu table and survey my accomplishments. My friend and right hand, Juliana de Oliveira, likes to remind me of the day we traveled on a crowded bus to São Paulo to buy tools at a kitchenware store for the Deville hotel kitchen we both worked for at the time. She says I predicted that, one day, I would go to that same store to purchase utensils for my own restaurant, and that I would earn respect and name recognition, and others would be curious about my recipes. On that same day, I predicted too that we would continue to work together—a dream come true. Success provides us a stage where we can lead by example, which of course carries its own set of responsibilities.

Today, I proudly wear the white chef's jacket to work. Gastronomy is not just part of my work life but in everything I breathe. Each night, my guests ring Manu's doorbell and are welcomed into the house, and I know we will serve them food with soul—dishes that tell the story of my heritage, that I enjoy eating, and, on a greater level, that support the local economy, minimum waste, and a passionate team of local producers. Here, we showcase ingredients of my land: molasses made with organic sugar cane, beets (beetroots) harvested during a full moon, and coffee grown by small producers. The best food is produced by people who love what they do. It's also local: we don't have to rely on much transport to obtain it.

I'll never forget the day one of my fish suppliers, Geovane Inácio from Inácio Pescados, had dinner with his wife at Manu. He was astounded by what we prepare with the fish and shells he carefully harvests for us every week. The thought of his smile helps me wake up on some lazy days. At the end of the night, it is not about the size of your restaurant; it's about strength, connections, hard work, and a strong desire to make the world a better place.

Ribeira River is located in the Ribeira Valley, where I source lemons, molasses, brown sugar, and cassava flour.

Native bees, fermentation, and acidic honey

Occasionally, Dario tells the story of the day I woke him up before 6 a.m. to go meet "someone special." We then picked up Sueli Alves da Silva, who announced we were about to meet some little bees. It was 2011, Manu had just opened, and I was organizing a dinner at a restaurant to explain how to cook with, and the benefits of, native Brazilian honey. Sueli was a coordinator at ACRIAPA (Associação de Criadores de Abelhas Nativas da Área de Proteção Ambiental de Guaraqueçaba/Association of Native Bee Breeders of the Guaraqueçaba Environmental Protection Area) and worked with native bees. At that time, native bee honey could not be sold due to dated legislation that a group of scientists and chefs (myself included) was trying to change. The acidity of honey from Brazilian native bees is higher than in *Apis mellifera* honey, which we used to source at markets, and its fermentation starts earlier than with most common honeys. According to this outdated law from 1953, this made it unsafe to preserve and sell. I was a fan of the ingredient, mainly *because* of its acidity and fermentation characteristics.

Let me give you a little background.

In the northern hemisphere, the most common bee is *Apis mellifera*, a species known to have a painful stinger. These bees live in colonies of between 60,000 and 80,000 bees, and produce most of the honey sold around the world. However, in the southern hemisphere (excluding Antarctica), there are said to be 500 types of stingless bees, living in significantly smaller colonies of between 300 and 900 bees. In fact, biologists have documented about 250 stingless bee species in Brazil alone. These bees build their hives in the hollows of old trees and are critical for crop and forest pollination. For example, in the state of Paraná, where I am from, these bees pollinate ninety per cent of flower species in the Atlantic Forest, which encompasses the entire Brazilian coast and approximately fifteen per cent of Brazil. They contribute to the higher crop yields and high-quality vegetables in the Atlantic Forest. This honey ferments quickly and has a unique sweetness that changes depending on the type of bee it's from. Some are floral; others have more or less accentuated acidity, depending on the time of the year they're produced.

Until the last thirty years, there were only a few keepers of stingless bees in Brazil. Today, there is a movement to increase native bee honey production and prevent these bees from becoming extinct. People are learning more about them and understanding what to do with their honey, which has medicinal uses. Each Brazilian region has its species of bees. For example, in South Brazil, we have mandaçaia, borá, and tubuna. In the north are tiúba and jupurá. Jataí is a species found across the entire country. They also form different hives from one another. One of the first things we noticed is how each has a different type of entrance to the hive.

Because of deforestation, some of these bees were at risk of extinction. This risk was especially high because, until about 2018, honey from these bees could not be traded. As a chef, I understood I could teach people to include honey from these stingless bees in their cooking routines and support a group of small producers trying to keep these bees alive and producing. The producers of Paraná worked hard to standardize the honey from native bees, and I've been fighting alongside them since 2011. My contribution to this battle is cooking with their honey, talking about them, and getting as many people interested in native bees as possible.

A few months after I opened Manu, I was introduced to Salete Perin and Benedito Uczai, who had just founded the Abelha Brasil project, which produces, jars, and sells honey from Paraná's native bees. In 2006, the couple, who had a homemade jam business, decided to take a course on meliponiculture—specifically, on keeping stingless indigenous bees—with the idea of improving the quality of the fruit trees they had on their property in Mandirituba, a city 25 miles (40 kilometers) from Curitiba. They then began cultivating bees of the mirim guaçu species. What started as a relaxing Sunday activity became their primary focus once they understood the difference the bees made to their fruit plantation: the fruit production increased by thirty per cent, and the fruit grew juicier, sweeter, and bigger.

Eventually, Salete and Benedito started researching other bee species and how each makes its hives, and structuring their production, including finding locations to cultivate the bees. They also opened up a market for the native bees, creating bottling options and a system for distribution. Today, they still grow delicious berries and herbs for their jams, but their main activity is keeping sixteen native bee species in their own forest. They have bee boxes at friends' small farms, too. In addition to cultivating bees in wooden boxes they built themselves, Benedito and Salete recover beehives and work toward the genetic renewal of native bees.

They were the ones who encouraged me to mount bee boxes on the exterior of Manu. I have mandaçaia, manduri, jataí, mirim guaçu, and mirim guaraipo bees, but only for pollination purposes; I do not take the honey from the boxes. I decided to have the boxes, here in the middle of the city, to educate people that our native bees are not dangerous and that anyone can have a box. I have three boxes at home, and the girls and I love watching the bees at work. Benedito visits my boxes from time to time. In 2021, he helped me get rid of lime native bees, a species of *Melipona* that doesn't produce honey and survives by invading other bees' hives and eating their food.

I've been cooking and talking about Brazilian native bees since shortly after I opened Manu. As a lover of acidity, I always look for ingredients that bring this flavor element to my recipes. Created in a humid environment, the stingless bees' honey is much more liquid than what we've known for a long time. Each kind of bee has certain enzymes that add flavor, aroma, density, and other qualities to its honey. For a chef, to have more than twenty kinds of honey to work with is fantastic. I've used these honeys with all sorts of dishes—fish, oysters, lamb, and various desserts. The native bees' honey is so complex and unique, and allows for such diverse preparation, that I could not imagine cooking without it.

The mirim saiqui bee honey, for example, is so acidic that it can be used like lime in some preparations. I love using it with fish and shellfish. The tubuna ones are full-bodied and go well with red meat. I combine them with raw meat, as they accentuate the earthy flavor. The yellow uruçu honey is simultaneously sweet and bitter. It goes well with duck magret, quail, boar, and other game meats. The jataí honey is acidic and fluid and has a beautiful golden color; I like to add some to the butter we use to marinate raw fish. Like cumin, cinnamon, sauces, and broths, honey from native Brazilian bees never misses in Manu's kitchen and is something that we constantly use for seasoning and creating new flavors.

A native guaraipo beehive.

Crayfish, crab, and tucum

In 2011, I was just starting my expeditions to find suppliers in Paraná. Some were in Santa Catarina, the state bordering Paraná to the north, others in Rio Grande do Sul, to the south. I never introduce an ingredient at Manu without knowing its provenance. My hope was that most of the products at Manu would come from within a radius of 185 miles (300 kilometers) of Curitiba. For this reason, I was on the road frequently for the first four years of the restaurant. Juliana had an old Corsa Wind Chevrolet that couldn't even do 60 miles (100 kilometers) per hour. We relied on it for many trips to North and South Paraná to find suitable products and producers. It was hard but fun.

My maternal grandparents were both born in Paranaguá, and we knew that the best of Paraná's seafood came from Paranaguá Bay, about 30 miles (50 kilometers) inland at the piedmont of the Serra do Mar mountain range. Mangrove swamps and marshes mainly fringe the interior of the bay, which has some small islands.

Between 2011 and 2015, I made the same trip every month. I'd wake up at 5 a.m., grab a coffee, and drive down the ocean highway, Serra da Graciosa, for one and a half hours until I reached the port city of Paranaguá. I would then take a boat for another hour to the community of Ponta do Laço on Ilha Rasa (Shallow Island).

All your problems are forgotten during that hour on the small motor boat making the crossing to Ilha Rasa. What a landscape! It is possible to count the more than fifty shades of green in the coastal vegetation. The sea is turquoise and transparent. More than eighty species of birds can be seen in the area. If you get lucky, you'll see some of the red birds. If not, you will notice about a dozen known aquatic species that dive into the waves and then appear a few meters ahead of the boat.

In remote areas with low-density populations, such as Ponta do Laço, everyone knows one another. Wilson, the boat driver, suggested I meet a man who knew practically everything about the region and was capable of building anything from scratch. This is how I came to buy vegetables, mussels, oysters, crayfish, and crab from Eriel "Nininho" Mendes and his wife, Tatiana "Tati" Paz da Silva.

It took me three visits to get an invitation to Nininho's home. He lives on an environmental reserve, and because of the size of my purse, he assumed I was a police officer or a tax inspector and was convinced I was there to kick him off the island. He lives in a conservation area that forbids newcomers—and in constant fear that someone will order him to leave his place. As soon as I saw his backyard, I understood we had to become friends. So I insisted. On my second visit, he accepted my business card. He then asked his younger daughter to research online whether I was a police officer and this way discovered I was a chef. The third time I showed up, he decided to give me a chance.

We both hit the lottery that afternoon. I told him about agroforestry and brought him seeds to grow. Everything he plants grows. He served the best oysters and crabs I've ever had, and he prepares them so simply. The quality of the product is so excellent that only water and salt are required for its preparation. Rice and beans are part of the Brazilian diet, the beans usually prepared with bacon and chunks of pork. Since there isn't any pork on the island, he usually makes his beans with oysters. Once the beans are soft, he seasons them with garlic, onions, and freshly caught oysters out of the shell. I remember eating his beans and then listening to the gears in my brain start to turn. I created one of the most famous dishes of Manu's first year after having lunch at Nininho's. He also had a fantastic variety of potato—known as tree trunk—that I used for a long time. And there was tucum, a small kind of coconut from a native palm tree, which we used to prepare a fermentation drink to welcome customers at Manu.

Nininho is a self-taught man who left school when he was nine years old to work at his father's liquor store. He is small but strong, with pale blue eyes, and knows every type of animal and plant on the island. He told me that the red-tailed Amazon parrots near his house don't fly on rainy days. Unlike the feathers of some birds, these parrots' feathers are not waterproof enough to withstand storms. I loved to arrive at Nininho's place after the rain to hear the sound of the more than 300 parrots that live there.

I always felt like a better person after spending time with Tati and Nininho. He built their house and everything in it. Tati takes care of it and does most of the cooking and cleaning. When I entered their home for the first time, I was intrigued by their oven. The door was an old car door. Nininho told me that Tati had wanted to make bread, and he needed the level of sealing a car door provided, so he got one from a junkyard on the island when making the kitchen appliance.

My partnership with Nininho lasted four years. My trips to Ilha Rasa ended as the restaurant began to work with new suppliers and I traveled more frequently across the country and abroad for my work. My team remembers me arriving on Fridays near opening time at the restaurant with incredible, never-before-seen fishes he had found for us. We learned a lot researching the best ways to prepare what he sent back with me. After a while, his son would bring their amazing products for me to Paranaguá Bay, so I didn't need to take the boat over. In exchange, I gave him seeds for plants Nininho still grows on his land—over sixty types all told. Today, he and Tati welcome university researchers from around the globe, as well as schoolchildren curious about this well-preserved area of the Atlantic Forest.

A fisherman harvesting native Brazilian oysters.

A view from Paranaguá Bay, where my maternal grandparents come from.

Molasses, peanuts, and cassava flour

"In your restaurant, you are the chef, and here I give the orders. Keep moving." This is how Divonei Mariano, owner of Vale e Cia (Valley and Co.), one of my producers, teases me every time I stir the molasses we use at Manu in his huge hand-me-down copper pot. (The pot is more than 3 feet/1 meter in diameter and holds 265 pounds/120 kilograms of *garapa*, or sugarcane liquid.) After cooking for seven hours over a wood fire, it reduces to about 21 quarts (20 liters). The final amount depends on the phase of the moon in which it is prepared. The last quarter moon is best for making molasses, but Divonei knows how to take advantage of each moon phase to get the best product possible.

In 2016, when I first met Divonei, I would visit his land at least five times a year to buy ingredients. He and his family eat what they cultivate—rice, beans, corn, vegetables, and fruits. They have chickens, pigs, and a small lake with fish, and they grow the best sugarcane I've ever tasted. Everything there is organic, and they rely on animals to pull equipment and old-fashioned mills to process the crops. They also respect the best moon phases for planting, harvesting, and dealing with the soil. For instance, they would never plant anything in the soil on the first Monday of a new moon—they say that nothing sprouts when planted on this day—something that has been observed for four generations. It was Divonei's grandfather who first established the family in that area and bought the plot.

Divonei and Nerli have two daughters, Debora and Dariane, both in their twenties, who help with the business while the parents manage production and the land. The women live in the small town of Cerro Azul, about 45 miles (70 kilometers) north of Curitiba. Divonei and Nerli make every effort not to leave the rural property at Bairro dos Macucos Road. Their agro-industry produces molasses, brown sugar, cassava, and many jams—orange, pumpkin, papaya, manioc zest, banana, and sweet potato. These are in addition to starch and flour, both derived from the cassava production chain. They also grow Ponkan tangerines, lemons, oranges, avocados, beans, corn, rice, and peanuts on the property.

I like to spend the day there. I eat the daily lunch, served on a large rectangular wooden table, on the veranda just outside the room where they prepare the molasses, and by the outdoor sink where they wash the cassava. It can be scorching hot on their farm, but there is always a nice breeze on the terrace, and we enjoy our meals with views of the mountains and crops. The food is prepared on a wood stove inside the house, in pots so clean you can see your reflection in them. The salad leaves are cut on a wooden board made by the family, then cleaned and hung on a wall to dry to avoid contamination. Everything in their wooden house is simple, clean, and tidy.

Divonei and Nerli are like family to me. At least twice a year, I do the three-hour journey on a curvy, one-lane scenic road to Cerro Azul, traveling another 10 miles (15 kilometers) or so on a dirt road until I arrive at their place. I always come home refreshed and feeling more creative after spending time with them. When there, I enjoy climbing a rock called *Pedra da panelada* (pan stone) on top of the mountain where Divonei grows the food. From there, you can see the vastness of the horizon. It reminds me of how beautiful the land is where I was born, how good its soil is, and how much we can learn from planting there.

The family's calm and beautiful way of dealing with life translates to everything they produce. And I love bringing it to Manu's table. It makes all the difference. The freshness of Divonei's peanuts is incredible, and their flavor is so nuanced in the peanut milk and other sauces we prepare with them. There is also a fresh cassava flour they sell exclusively to me, which all started when I took my daughter Helena there for the first time. Nerli was grating the freshly peeled cassava, and Helena began eating it from the pot.

She could not stop eating it, which gave me the idea of finishing the flour myself at the restaurant. Nerli calls this fresh flour *raspa de mandioca* (cassava zest). She sometimes uses it in desserts. Most of the time, after grating, she roasts it to get the cassava flour. Since we have such a good relationship, they agreed to sell me the unfinished cassava zest. It is one of my secret ingredients. I take it fresh, and we finish it in various ways at Manu. I love when we roast it with lard. The crunchiness of Divonei's cassava flour is unmatched. Vanessa, who runs the restaurant's dessert program, loves working with it. She and Helena are the ones who make the most extensive shopping list each time I travel to Cerro Azul. And I love to drive back home thinking of the smiles they both will give me when I show them my purchases.

Cups, cafés, and petit fours

Sometimes, when you open your front door, you unlock goodwill and pleasant surprises come your way. The master coffee roaster Cláudia Bentlin first walked through the doors at Manu because of my ceramics. As with everything else at Manu, I care about what dishware we use to serve our food and drinks. We eat with our eyes first. I love finding good ceramists, and I've even developed restaurant dishes with some of them. Our team has private names for each of our plate types. There is the cone-shaped "volcano," which resembles that eruptive force of nature; the "cat" and "dog" plates, which look like pets' water bowls; the "octopus," which resembles the texture of those eight-legged cephalopods, and so on. When we ask our front-of-house team—Deibd Rodrigues, Emiliano Lauriano, and Jean Santana—for a certain plate using its nickname, they know exactly which to bring us.

One of my favorite discoveries, in 2017, were the cups with legs, made by a journalist-photographer couple who moved from Curitiba to the Paraná countryside and opened a ceramist studio called Boitatá (after the mythological creature that, according to Indigenous peoples, lives in and protects the forest). When Cláudia saw that I used these beautiful ceramics for serving coffee, she told me rather bluntly that she liked the restaurant very much but felt that our coffee service could be better. I've always been a coffee enthusiast. I truly wake up only after having my first sip of hot coffee. Brazil, a nation of coffee fans, could do much better in terms of the quality of the coffee consumed. Our country is the largest coffee producer globally, and for years Paraná was the most prominent area for coffee production in the country. My grandpa Eduardo grew coffee on his farm. But in 1975, black frost destroyed the roots and leaves of plants at coffee plantations across the state, and it lost its lead when many farmers, my grandfather included, gave up growing coffee plants. I knew the coffee at the restaurant was okay, but I understood that she was referring to the bigger picture.

For more than ten years, Cláudia worked as a bank employee in the Curitiba city center. She would drink espresso two or three times a day, frequenting the numerous coffee shops in the area. Of course, she preferred some cups over others. Eventually, she decided to train as a barista and discovered she had special sensory ability. Having left the bank, she started earning her living as a coffee professional and joined the Specialty Coffee Association of America (SCAA), a non-profit, membership-based organization representing thousands of coffee professionals, from producers to baristas, around the world. The SCAA evaluates the drink on a scale of from zero to 100 points, with a margin of error of two percentage points. To earn the title of "specialty," the coffee needs to score between eighty and 100. Cláudia now owns a small café in Curitiba, the Distinto Café, and visits producers and evaluates coffee in various parts of Paraná and around Brazil. At her café, she works only with grounds that achieve at least eighty-two points on the SCAA scale.

My initial meeting with Cláudia was a case of love at first chat. From that moment, I started a new path in coffee service. Everything started with a blind tasting, where she presented me with six varieties of coffee in six identical transparent cups. My daughter Helena was still quite young at the time, and she was with me that day. Cláudia prepared a special place for her, with three cups. Helena enjoyed smelling the roasted coffee beans, waiting for the liquid of the brewed coffee to settle, breaking the drink's crust, sampling it, and spitting the rest out into a paper cup. When we finished the test, the coffee I liked most was the one Cláudia had expected me to work with. It was a bean produced in Ribeirão Claro, a traditional coffee area in North Paraná that borders the state of São Paulo. The coffee was super acidic and suited my taste buds. Cláudia invited Helena to fill the box for the first bespoke coffee roast for Manu.

After choosing the coffee, Cláudia invited us to visit the farm where these unique beans are produced. We stayed on this century-old farm, a coffee producer in Paraná's golden years but now serving as a guesthouse for those interested in the drink. The farmers grow coffee for home consumption and know a lot about the region and its producers. I went with Dario and the girls, and still cherish the memory of those beautiful days full of learning.

To work with this unique coffee, I had to change the petit fours that finished off the meal at Manu. The coffee did not go well with gluten, so we developed a coconut cookie very different from the butter cookies we were serving. We also created a chocolate cookie with 69% dark chocolate from the Amazonia region. We started making a brigadeiro (a Brazilian truffle) with boiled milk and brown sugar instead of with condensed milk, since chocolate and the coffee blend perfectly. We even had cheese and peanut cookies to accompany our special coffee.

Cláudia proposed I buy a bag of coffee a year (each bag contains 132 pounds/60 kilograms of green beans, more or less the amount needed for a year's service at the restaurant) and change the producer after a full year. This way, I would get to know different quality suppliers. She roasts our coffee twice a week, so we serve freshly roasted coffee every day. We also started filtering the coffee in front of the client so they could smell the high-quality drink being prepared. It is priceless. I do believe coffee is how restaurant service should conclude.

Since 2019, I've bought coffee only through Cláudia and only from female producers in Paraná. All the beans are hand-harvested and planted in organic conditions, according to the best moon phases and weather conditions. Each selected coffee has a unique taste and aroma. Being creative is also about serving something unexpected. Our coffee has its charm and may look and be prepared like coffee, but it can taste more like hibiscus tea or raspberries.

A recent batch of beans we served was produced by Ariele Miranda Afonso. The first time she left her hometown of Curiúva (also in North Paraná) was to visit Cláudia's coffee shop in Curitiba. She was amazed to see how her beans were prepared and served. I am touched to hear so many beautiful stories about the food—and drink—we serve. I also have special affection for the coffee we served in 2021. It was from Terezinha das Graças Rodrigues, who died after selling her first bag to me. Her coffee was sweeter than what I've used before and had a light acidity. I was the only restaurateur to use the coffee of this extraordinary woman who created the Mulheres do Café (Women in Coffee) project to encourage young women farmers from the Pinhalão region to produce coffee. Pinhalão too is in North Paraná, relatively close to Montes Claros. I remember watching her filter coffee for us, over a white wood stove, in her clean, white kitchen and chatting away in her thick, sweet accent. That day, she told me to never give up on my dreams, no matter my age. Terezinha realized a dream of becoming a coffee producer at age seventy and said she was happier in a way she had never imagined. I learned it's never too late to take the first step in that kitchen.

Umami and wild mushrooms

In 2017, I first heard about people foraging for wild mushrooms in Santa Catarina and the Rio Grande do Sul's forests. Brazilian people were not used to consuming mushrooms. According to statistics from the Brazilian Association of Mushroom Producers, Brazilians eat fewer than 100 grams of them per person each year. In the United States, annual consumption per capita in 2020 was about 6.5 pounds (3 kilograms). In Europe, this number varies from 4.5 to 6.5 pounds (2 to 3 kilograms) per year depending on the country. And in Asia, people eat between about 11 and 13 pounds (5 and 6 kilograms) in a year. The portobello is the most popular mushroom in Brazil, and for years we could only find them already boiled and packaged in glasses or cans—never fresh. They were called "champignons," the French word for mushrooms. Italian restaurants in Brazil make recipes with dried porcini and, when Japanese food became popular in around 2000, shimeji and shiitake were integrated into Brazilian kitchens. The state of São Paulo is the largest planted-mushroom producer, with 500 mushroom farmers, which is nothing compared with the more than 20,000 tomato producers in the area (a Brazilian eats about 10 pounds/4 kilograms of tomatoes a year).

I am a huge fan of mushrooms, and I was fascinated to learn that they are neither animals nor plants but fungi, and have been on the planet since the time of the dinosaurs. Mushrooms are one of the most nutrient-dense foods in the world, with high levels of protein, minerals, fiber, and vitamin D. They are also rich in umami, the fifth basic taste alongside sour, sweet, bitter, and salty. One translation of the Japanese word *umami* is "essence of deliciousness." I always add umami to my dishes, and mushrooms are a good source.

In 2018, I met Francisco, who taught me about the mushrooms I would find in Santa Catarina and Paraná. A few months later, I traveled to Serra Dona Francisca, a 260-mile (420-kilometer) pine-forested road that connects the north of Santa Catarina to the coast, to hunt porcini mushrooms with chef Willian Vieira, who is familiar with that part of the state. Santa Catarina is a neighboring state to South Paraná.

I was raised to be in touch with nature and do my best to ensure my girls are also. Helena was already two years old, so we all woke up just before dawn on Saturday to drive to the mountain region of Santa Catarina. We arrived at around 8 a.m. and walked into the pine forest, with its distinct scent, closed canopy, and relatively little understory. I like to hear the sound of the forest and my feet crunching on the dry pine needles as I walk. I became emotional seeing my little daughter walk on that pine-needle floor.

Willian runs a restaurant based on local ingredients and knows where to find the mushrooms. It was the middle of fall (autumn), we had had a rainy spring, and there were plenty of them around. You have to gently make some space among the fallen leaves to see the rounded whitish dome of the mushrooms, but once your eyes are trained, you'll spot them everywhere. Helena quickly understood how it worked and got excited about finding the porcini. At first, she would find them and wait for me to arrive to collect them. After watching us several times, she started making space around the mushrooms so she too could pull the stem very close to the ground. Once she had one in her hand, she would run to me and ask me to clean the soil around the base with the little knife I had on me. We stayed there the entire morning.

We returned from that first hunt with more than 45 pounds (20 kilograms) of mushrooms. Dried mushrooms have much more umami than fresh ones, so we dehydrated almost all of them, though I saved some fresh ones to serve on the vegetarian menu. I also used some to make the powder that finishes many Manu preparations. Some go back to the pot to become a super-rich umami broth that I thicken with tapioca and use in certain recipes; some I add to Manu's demi-glace. The bread I serve to start the menu contains mushrooms, and sometimes I make mushroom butter.

Boletus edulis is a porcini that grows in pine forests at over 3,280 feet (1,000 meters) in southern Brazil. The Brazilian mushrooms have the same fleshiness as the Italian ones but with a slightly lighter aroma because of our terroir. In recent years, porcini hunting has become somewhat of a trend in Santa Catarina and Paraná—many chefs have become mushroom hunters and even organize tours with gourmands who want to learn how to forage and prepare them.

After a few trips to Serra Dona Francisca with Willian, from whom I learned to recognize edible mushrooms and avoid poisonous ones, I started to hunt mushrooms by myself. Besides porcini, I find a lot of the *Lactarius* species as well. They also have a rounded dome, but the inside is all gills. There are *Lactarius* and mini *Lactarius* in the pine forests I visit—even in the one nearby my house in Pinhais or at my husband's family farm in Cantagalo, a Paraná city 200 miles (320 kilometers) west of Curitiba. My girls and my team love mushroom-hunting days. It is best to arrive early in the morning, to have more light for the long hunts. Now, we never finish the adventure with less than 65 pounds (30 kilograms) of mushrooms. Both my girls know that the red mushrooms with white spots, the amanita, cannot be collected. Back home at the dining table with Dario and the girls, enjoying a dish we've prepared with the mushrooms we foraged, we talk excitedly about their flavor, size, and how easy or difficult it was to find them.

Oysters, crabs, and white mussels

Anyone looking at a map of the Brazilian coast will notice that the state of Paraná has the second-smallest coastal area in the country. The first is Piauí's, at the far north of the country's coastline. Brazil is surrounded on its eastern coast by the Atlantic Ocean and has more than 4,970 miles (8,000 kilometers) of beach, 60 miles (95 kilometers) of which are in Paraná. Paraná's coast is full of bays, and, as a result, the sea is muddy and shallow, with an extensive mangrove where we find blue crab, Atlantic ghost crab, soft shell crab, and amazing native oysters. For this, I travel a little further south to Florianópolis, in Santa Catarina, my favorite summer destination for deep sea fish. In addition, we can also find great shrimp (prawn) and native oyster farms in Santa Catarina's open sea. My white mussels come from Rio Grande do Sul's beaches, even further south.

As Brazilian home cooking tends to be meat-based, Brazilians eat very little fish. The last poll released in 2020 by the fisheries ministry revealed that Brazilians consume about 22 pounds (10 kilograms) of fish per year. It is less than half of the meat consumption, which is 54.2 pounds (24.6 kilograms) according to a 2021 study coordinated by the Associação Brasileira de Proteína Animal (Brazilian Association of Animal Protein). Despite our immense coastline, the river fish are famous here. A curious fact is that the people of the Amazon, which is entirely landlocked, eat twice as much fish as the rest of the country's inhabitants. The Indigenous people have an expression: "Thank the gods we have the fish to enjoy our cassava flour with."

It's been more than a decade since I spent every New Year's Eve with my mom in Florianópolis. She was raised by the sea and makes no compromises: a good year starts by the sea. The Buffara family knows how to prepare seafood, so I grew up appreciating it. Besides that, during my gap year, I spent a month on a fishing boat in Alaska and became pretty good at preparing halibut.

The scallops and some of the oyster varieties I serve at the restaurant are produced at Vinicius Ramos's Paraíso das Ostras (Oysters' Paradise), an oyster farm at the southern end of Florianópolis. With the most renowned beach in South Brazil, Florianópolis is an island with an open sea area perfect for growing oysters. Vinicius and his family live and work in the south of the island, where they grow incredible oysters and scallops. They receive the oysters' seeds, work closely with the researchers of the Universidade Federal de Santa Catarina (Federal University of Santa Catarina), and have the tidiest, cleanest, and most organized process of oyster cultivation in the state. It's always a pleasure to visit Vinicius and observe how carefully he deals with his production. No wonder his oysters are elegant, fleshy, and subtle. They taste like a clean ocean. In addition to being fresh, the scallops, with perfect texture and appearance, come in an impeccable shell.

Paraná also has an incredible native oyster grower, Nereu de Oliveira. He cultivates the best native oysters in the state. Before I became allergic to oysters and could no longer eat them, I longed for these the most. This oyster is small and has a pronounced and consistent flavor. It also has that punch I look forward to when designing a dish.

I love to scuba dive and snorkel. My brother and daughters always pay close attention when diving with me. I get hypnotized by that big underwater world and easily drift out to sea, so my partner's role is to rescue me. Whenever I go diving, I ask if it is possible to catch clams, urchins, or other shells. I like to harvest myself what I bring to the table. My daughters love to do this, too.

As we do with mushrooms, I sometimes go hunting for seaweed with them and anyone else who wants to come along. One of the first times I went was with Willian Vieira from Santa Catarina (page 107). We spotted loads of sea lettuce and samphire that I brought to the restaurant, dehydrated, and made into a powder that I use as a seasoning or add to the fish cure. Some unconventional food plants can be found in wild beach areas, like an orange orchid that tastes like melon, and certain leaves that I sometimes use to finish dishes.

I'm devoted to hyperlocal and sustainable ingredients, including seafood. I cook with only fresh fish and shellfish, and I was trained to recognize the best. Fresh fish smells like the sea and has lively eyes and a firm texture. If you press on a fresh fish, the skin will bounce back right away. The skin must be shiny, with well-attached scales, and the gills must be pink. Fish with dull eyes and greenish or slimy gills are not fresh. The smell of ammonia, or a very strong fish smell is also a bad sign. Shrimp (prawn) meat should also be firm. I serve scallops at Manu only because I finally met the best supplier, after extensive research. They are very delicate and can spoil quickly, and they will lose their sweetness, moisture, and shine if transported or packaged improperly.

When I opened Manu, I traveled twice a month to Paranaguá Bay to guarantee fresh fish at the restaurant. I met the fishers myself to be sure I was serving the fish of the day. My team often hears me say not to kill the ingredient twice. I'm bold when it comes to the perfect cook point of my dishes: I've worked with experienced chefs who overcook my recipes. I like to think outside the box, and I propose different textures. I work with the whole fish, with belly and scales. We clean the fish at the house, remove the fillet, and cure it. I use an old curing technique: equal parts of salt and sugar are spread over the fish, which is then placed on a rack and in the refrigerator.

Now I have fish from dependable suppliers, such as Bernardo Fuck of Trapiche Pescados, and Geovane Inácio of Inácio Pescados (page 92). Geovane sends me a picture of the fishing boat arriving with products he will bring me in a few hours. He always comes to the restaurant with his feet dirty with sand from the beach. He tells me if the fish is fat and if the shells are good. He also presents me with new options from time to time, such as the white mussels that I included in my Metamorphosis menu (page 53), served in 2021. These cold-water mussels are naturally white and can be found in the very southern part of Brazil, Argentina, and Uruguay.

They used to be highly appreciated by fishers who steamed them with garlic and parsley. According to Geovane, few locals were buying them, so there was a lot left on the fishing boats. I was amazed when I received them, and it was easy to create something to go well with these gifts of the sea. Other fish suppliers started receiving orders for white mussels from us. Since they did not know that specific species, they were puzzled and said it was impossible to assure the mussel inside the shell was white. It took a long time for them to realize which mussel I was serving and where they come from.

Hampshire Down lambs, at Fazenda Ferrador, provide the restaurant with sustainable, organic meat.

Lamb, Moura pig, and the perfect carrot

In southern Brazil, where I was born and raised, it is common to barbecue typically beef—on Sundays. And on that day, the father of the family traditionally takes care of the food. It is rare for women to helm the barbecue. But my father cooks nothing—not even barbecue—and I was never fond of beef. It was easy for me to erase beef from Manu's menu, in 2019. I use pork or lamb, but no longer beef. Even working with premium-quality cuts, I serve only one dish of red meat—lamb or pork—on our menu.

In the late 1990s, researchers at Universidade Federal do Paraná (Federal University of Paraná) studied the Moura pig (*porco Moura*), a pig native to Brazil and a hybrid of a local species and a species brought by the Spanish Jesuit priests between 1500 and 1700. They were at risk of extinction, but the researchers managed to prevent this fate, though it took a while for a farmer to develop good Moura pig products for chefs. It is not really an option to buy the whole pig for a restaurant as small as Manu: we do not have uses for all the pig parts, and I am against waste in my kitchen. But then I learned of Felipe Nicolau Soifer, of Casa Gralha Azul (Blue Parrot House). His free-range pigs eat organic vegetables, seeds, and various types of pumpkin. They are fantastic, and he sells the parts to different food producers. I use his pork meat, lard, and a guanciale (cured bacon from the pig cheek) from a reliable Curitiba sausage house that uses Casa Gralha Azul pork.

My lamb comes from a farm to which I have a solid emotional connection. My aunt Rosane Garmatter Buffara, married to my mother's brother, Nelson Buffara Junior, raises the lamb. She is a small-scale producer, working only with crosses of Hampshire Down (the best-marbled meat) and Ile de France (which is the perfect size) and Texel (the best carcass shape for meat) species. The meat she produces is unique. Aunt Rosane herself takes care of every detail of the sheep's feeding, care, and slaughtering. She will wake up in the middle of the night when the sheep are being born to ensure everything is going smoothly with the deliveries, and she will bottle-feed the newborns if necessary. They are then raised at the farm of her father, Fazenda Ferrador, where I spent some unforgettable holidays and where I like to escape for a home-cooked lunch and good conversation every now and then. I am so confident in the quality of her meat that I dare serve it rarer than usual, for those customers who are delighted to try it.

Manu's menu is very flexible. Considering the season, I create a range of plates that fit the menu. This way, I always have an option if the carrots aren't good that day or if the octopus is not the best I can get that week. There are times my team calls me, saying, "We have too much squid ink in the freezer." It's not a problem for me—I will create something that uses it perfectly.

The quality of the fish or shellfish I receive every day makes it impossible not to create something from it. In fact, on some of our menus, you'll find six seafood dishes.

Some of my best dishes have arisen from clients' dietary restrictions. For a while, I did not offer many vegetarian or vegan recipes. My sous-chef Debora Teixeira, who has been with me since before Manu, takes good care of our daily mise en place. She guarantees that what we've planned is always there, in the right proportion, texture, color, and taste. And I can improvise around it. Our sauces, broths, fermentations, and other preparations are so well developed that creating a new last-minute dish is often a nice challenge. I was already in love with cauliflower when I had to improvise a vegan dish using it. Cauliflower can have a strong taste or no taste, depending on how you prepare it. Its flower-like appearance also captivates me. Our cauliflower and bottarga dish was already a hit, but to make it vegan, I used cashew milk instead of bottarga. It was so good that we later included it on the main menu. I also developed a vegetarian version with a homemade cauliflower-and-passion-fruit butter served alongside the fried cauliflower (page 200). The umami that comes from this preparation is incredible. I love passion fruit, and it shows up in different ways in my recipes.

One remarkable dish I serve in Curitiba is based on a dish I created when cooking at a hotel in the Maldives. One guest couldn't eat raw food, and I had raw shrimp (prawn) on the menu. I asked the chef if he had fresh leeks, and he did, so I steamed them. Then I asked for peanuts, tomatoes, cumin, onions, soy sauce, lemongrass, coriander, and chives. I sautéed everything together and processed the mixture into a thick sauce. I then seasoned almond milk with lime. Since I had a dish with crayfish, I used its head to prepare a bisque sauce. The resulting dish was steamed leek with a little of all these preparations.

I always dreamed of having a carrot dish. When I was young, I competed in equestrian competitions, and I remain fond of horses to this day. We fed the horses with carrots, and I sometimes ate them myself. Since then, I've learned a lot about this root vegetable, but it took me years to create a carrot dish. Whenever my team rates my creation as good, nice, okay, or interesting, I throw it in the trash. I want my food to be extraordinary and to arouse emotions. And this was challenging to do with a carrot.

I appreciate the umami from fermented preparations. One afternoon while making sourdough bread, I decided to make an accompanying sauce, thickening it with butter. Funnily enough, my first thought was to cook the sauce in a vacuum, but since it was fermented, it exploded. (Sometimes, our kitchen exploits resemble science experiments.) We persisted with the idea of the vacuum, deciding to put less sauce in the bag and adding soy sauce, garlic, and tucupi. And *a-ha*! We had the perfect fermented sauce. But there was just one problem: nothing went well with it.

I was still looking for the perfect cook point for the carrot. Sure, the carrot itself was already special: it was organic and harvested during a crescent moon, when it is sweetest. I did not want it to be al dente; it had to be soft while maintaining its structure. We washed it carefully and left it unpeeled in an attempt to retain the carrot's integrity. Then we steamed it for eight minutes. I like cumin, which is not used much in Brazilian kitchens. I mixed together some red and black pepper, cumin leaf and seeds, and coriander seeds, then massaged the steamed carrot with the rub. It was grilled (griddled) on the barbecue to add smokiness and then served with the fermented sauce (page 74).

The dish surprises. There is a lot of butter in the sauce, so it is easy to understand that part of it. But then you're perplexed by the carrot's texture and the taste of leaven. I am proud to finish a menu with this dish. Instead of serving the final meat, I send out this carrot. I like to talk about the two or three dishes everyone remembers after eating a menu I prepare. The carrot is often among them, which makes me extremely happy.

Working with carrot and cauliflower helped me understand that I don't want too many things on the plate. I want to simplify the dish but still bring all the flavors and textures an ingredient can offer. I like spicy food, but each herb or seed has a role on a plate I create. To cook well is much more than having the best recipe. It's about understanding each ingredient and creating the best moment for it. I love to think of myself as a fashion designer who has to find the best outfit for each ingredient I receive. Once I followed that path, I was freer to improvise.

Imagination

Here we have the combination of ideas, images, and daydreams. Imagination represents my mind's digressions—conceiving an imaginary world and creating innovative combinations beyond our reality. It enriches the spirit and allows me freedom.

Mushroom brioche with pork ointment and Manu's butter

My food defines my philosophy and tells my story. My grandmother always stressed the importance of tactility—for example, to touch bread dough and feel the fermentation with our hands—and time. Precision timing is critical for our fermentation at Manu. The patience in preparing bread over two days is what makes our brioche so special.

I developed the pork ointment when I opened Manu, and it has been served since day one. When I created the first menu at Manu, I knew the bread moment had to be unique. My mother always says that a meal will be good if the bread arrives at the table in good shape and tastes delicious. I'm a fan of bread with lard, so besides serving the best bread I could, I also created a special spread to go with it. This pork ointment is so appreciated by the guests that it has always been in the restaurant service.

I've always loved butter and so decided to make my own for the restaurant (page 179). The butter recipe is the foundation of the many versions.

Makes 6 brioches

For Manu's butter	1 L heavy (double) cream
	500 g plain (natural) yogurt
	fleur de sel, for sprinkling
For the pork ointment	150 g lard
	75 g cubed bacon
	50 g onion, brunoise
	9 g garlic
	60 g roasted peanuts
	11 g cilantro (coriander) leaves
	3 g salt
	1 g black pepper
For the mushroom brioche Part 1	250 g white (button) mushrooms
	75 g butter
Part 2	75 g bread flour
	57 ml water
	2 g fresh yeast
Part 3	302 g all-purpose (plain) flour, plus extra for dusting
	94 ml water
	94 g lightly beaten eggs
	45 ml honey
	8 g salt
	113 g room-temperature brown butter (beurre noisette)
Part 4	60 g egg
	10 ml heavy (double) cream
	0.02 g salt

Manu's butter In a bowl, lightly mix the cream with the yogurt. Cover with cheesecloth (muslin) and ferment at room temperature for at 48 hours, until the cream curdles and it smells acidic—the time depends on the room's temperature. Place the mixture in the refrigerator to chill for 12 hours.

Transfer the mixture to the bowl of a stand mixer fitted with the paddle attachment. Beat on medium speed, increasing the speed gradually, until the mixture first comes together, then separates into solids and whey. Strain the mixture through a chinois to drain the whey (which can be used in other recipes) from the butter. Place the butter in a bowl in an ice bath and gently work it with a rubber spatula to remove all traces of whey. Refrigerate until firm.

Pork ointment Cook the lard in a skillet over low heat, ensuring the temperature stays below 122°F (50°C). Add the bacon and cook down for 2 hours, until golden. Add the onion and garlic and sauté for 10 minutes. Stir in the peanuts. Transfer the mixture to a Thermomix and mix on high speed until pureed. Add the cilantro (coriander) and mix for 2 minutes. Add the salt and pepper and mix again. Set aside to cool to room temperature.

Mushroom brioche Part 1 Clean the mushrooms, then place them in the food processor and process well. Melt the butter in a skillet over medium heat. Stir in the mushrooms to coat in the butter. Reduce the heat to low and cook for at least 1 hour, stirring occasionally, until the mushrooms are golden and paste-like in texture and have released all their moisture. Let cool, then transfer to a pastry bag. Refrigerate until needed.

Part 2 Using your hands, combine the flour, water, and yeast in a bowl to develop minimal gluten. Set aside to ferment for 4 hours at room temperature.

Part 3 Put the flour in a bowl and make a well in the center. Add the water, eggs, honey, salt, and fermented sponge. Mix the wet ingredients together quickly, then stir in half of the flour and mix well. Stir in the remaining flour. Knead the dough for 3 minutes until gluten is developed and the dough pulls away from your hands. Add the brown butter (beurre noisette) little by little, incorporating it into the dough until homogeneous. Let the dough rest for 15 minutes in a bowl, covered with plastic wrap (clingfilm).

Make the first fold of the bread: holding the dough at one side, pull it up and fold it over itself. Repeat this fold on the remaining 3 sides of the dough. Rest at room temperature for another 15 minutes. Do a second round of folding.

Rest the dough at room temperature in a covered container for 16 hours. Then refrigerate the dough for 8 hours to cool and slow down the fermentation.

Place the dough on a lightly floured work surface. Using a rolling pin, roll the dough into a 12- × 17¾-inch (30- × 45-cm) rectangle, about ¼ inch (5 mm) thick. Using a spatula, spread an even layer of the mushroom paste over the dough. Fold the dough like an envelope, bringing the bottom corners inward and covering two-thirds of the dough. Take the ends from top to bottom, covering the other part and forming the envelope. Roll out the dough again, stretching it slightly to the sides. Cut the dough into 6 rectangles. In one of the rectangles, make 2 incisions lengthwise, leaving ¾ inch (2 cm) at the base, forming 3 strips from each piece. Braid the strips together, then join the ends, creating a rounded shape. Repeat with the remaining dough rectangles.

Place the brioches on a greased and lightly floured baking sheet. Set the dough aside for 5 hours at a temperature of 73°F (23°C).

Part 4 Whisk all the ingredients together in a bowl to make an egg wash, taking care to not add too much air to the mixture.

Preheat the oven to 350°F (180°C). Brush a thin film of egg wash over the brioches. Bake for 10 minutes. Reduce the temperature to 325°F (160°C) and bake for another 15 minutes, or until golden. Place brioches on a wire rack to cool.

To serve Finish the chilled butter with fleur de sel and serve alongside the cooled brioches and pork ointment.

Fish, citrus, and saiqui honey

Mirim saiqui, a species of native Brazilian bee, can be found in well-preserved forests on the hillsides and mountains. Sweet yet highly acidic, the honey from this bee pairs perfectly with raw fish, very strong coconut milk, and Brazilian cashew nuts, found across the country's northeast coast.

Serves 4

For the fish	0.5 g sugar
	0.5 g fine pink salt
	200 g sea bass loin
For the citruses	150 g grapefruit
	140 g navel orange
	100 g lemon
	80 g lime
For the cashew nut milk	100 g cashew nuts
	100 ml Coconut Milk (see page 68)
	100 ml tucupi
	5 ml rice vinegar
	5 g salt
For the cashew crunch	50 g cashew nuts
	10 ml olive oil
	5 g pimenta de cheiro (green chile pepper), chopped
	5 g salt
	2 g black pepper
To serve	10 ml saiqui native bee honey
	3 g fleur de sel

Fish   Combine the sugar and salt in a small bowl. Season the fish all over with the cure and let it rest on a wire rack over a rimmed baking sheet for at least 4 hours, uncovered, in the refrigerator. Then pat dry with paper towel, cover, and refrigerate until needed.

Citruses   Segment the citrus fruits. Set aside.

Cashew nut milk   Combine the cashews, coconut milk, and tucupi in a Thermomix and mix on high speed for 8 minutes until smooth and homogeneous. Strain the mixture through a chinois into a bowl. Season with vinegar and salt. Refrigerate until needed.

Cashew crunch   Chop the cashews into small pieces. Place in a bowl, then season with olive oil, chile, salt, and pepper.

To serve   Thinly slice the fish as if for sashimi or carpaccio. Arrange the fish on plates and drizzle the saiqui honey overtop. Arrange 2 slices of each citrus among the fish slices. Sprinkle over 2 teaspoons of cashew crunch and top with a few drops of cashew nut milk. Finish with the fleur de sel.

Shrimp, pork, and onion

I sometimes travel to the Brazilian coast to harvest the bounty of samphire, but there are several good local samphire suppliers in Curitiba. I love to cure shrimp (prawns) in a samphire powder that I make—it lends delicacy to the shrimp meat. Pancetta oil balances the recipe. The remaining ingredients add flavor and textures to the dish.

Serves 4

For the shrimp	30 g sugar
	15 g salt
	15 g dehydrated samphire
	200 g peeled and deveined fresh shrimp (prawns)

For the green marinade	500 ml tucupi
	100 g dill
	50 g Italian parsley
	50 g cilantro (coriander) leaves
	25 g lemongrass
	15 g pimenta de cheiro (green chile pepper)
	10 g peeled ginger
	300 ml Cashew Nut Oil (see page 142)
	3 garlic cloves (without the middle part)

For the pancetta oil	200 g pancetta
	5 g rosemary leaves
	5 g ground cumin
	1 g ground cinnamon
	1 g white pepper

| For the crispy onion | 700 ml vegetable oil |
| | 200 g white onion, finely sliced |

| To serve | 3 g purple oxalis sprouts |

Shrimp In a bowl, combine the sugar, salt, and samphire until well mixed. Toss the shrimp (prawns) with the mixture, then place on a wire rack set over a rimmed baking sheet. Cure in the refrigerator at 40°F (5°C) for 8 hours.

Green marinade Blend all the ingredients in a blender on high speed for 8 minutes. Strain the mixture through a chinois and refrigerate until needed.

Pancetta oil Cut the pancetta into 2-inch (5-cm) cubes. Place in a skillet, add the remaining ingredients, and render over medium heat for 30 minutes. Strain, then set it aside.

Crispy onion Heat the oil in a saucepan over medium-low heat. Add the onion and deep-fry for 40 minutes, or until golden brown. Drain, then transfer to a plate lined with paper towel to drain further. Transfer to a tray and dehydrate at 167°F (75°C) for 30 minutes, or until crispy.

To serve Cut the shrimp into ½-inch (1-cm) cubes. Gently toss with the green marinade to coat. Let rest for 2 hours at room temperature. Spread a layer of shrimp in the center of each flat plate. Drizzle over the warm pancetta oil, top with the crispy onion, and finish with the oxalis sprouts.

Zucchini, native honey, and flowers

The simplicity of zucchini (courgette), common on the kitchen tables of many Brazilian homes, does not prevent it from being a great ingredient with many possibilities.

Serves 4

For the creamy fish stock
80 ml vegetable oil
30 g sliced ginger
7 g smashed ginger
500 g grouper or yellowtail with bones
2 L boiling water

For the rice noodle soup
100 g mixed mushrooms
3 slices cucumber
3 slices tomato
2 pan-fried crispy tofu
small bunch of beansprouts
700 ml Creamy Fish Stock (see above)
300 g rice noodles, presoaked in warm water until softened
10 ml light soy sauce
2.5 g white pepper
salt, to season

For the zucchini (courgette)
35 g butter
10 g onion, brunoise
8 g grated ginger
3 g garlic, brunoise
10 g cambuci pepper, brunoise
350 g sliced zucchini (courgette)
15 ml tucupi
100 ml Rice Noodle Soup stock (see above)
100 ml Coconut Milk (see page 68)
100 g sorrel leaves
5 g salt
1 hydrated gelatin sheet

To serve
10 ml tubuna native bee honey
edible flower petals

Creamy fish stock Heat the oil in a large saucepan over medium heat. Add the ginger and cook for 3 minutes. Add the fish and sauté for 30 minutes, or until slightly browned. Break up the fish into small pieces. Add the boiling water, cover, and cook for 65 minutes. Using a fine strainer, strain the stock and remove any small bones.

Rice noodle soup In a large saucepan, place the mushrooms, cucumber, tomato, pan-fried tofu, and beansprouts. Pour in the creamy fish stock and bring to a boil. Add the soaked rice noodles, then season with soy sauce, white pepper, and salt. Cook for 1 minute. Strain the stock and set aside.

Zucchini Heat the butter in a skillet over medium heat until lightly browned. Add the onion and sauté for 30 minutes. Add the ginger and garlic and sauté for 3 minutes, or until fragrant. Add the cambuci pepper and zucchini (courgette) and cook over low heat for 30 minutes, or until the zucchini is very soft.

Add the tucupi, stock from the rice noodle soup, and coconut milk and gently boil over low heat for another 15 minutes. Transfer the mixture to a Thermomix, add the sorrel, and mix on high speed for 5 minutes. Strain the mixture through a chinois into a saucepan. Bring to a gentle heat, season with salt, and stir in the hydrated gelatin to dissolve. Strain through the chinois again to make sure the mixture is smooth. Pour into a 500-ml siphon, close, and insert 2 charges. Refrigerate for at least 4 hours before serving.

To serve Put the zucchini foam in a snack dish. Drizzle with the tubuna honey and top with the edible flower petals. Serve immediately.

Oyster, leek, and thyme oil

I always have leek and thyme in the kitchen—both at home and in the restaurant. Whenever I receive a sizeable quantity of quality oysters, I try to find a way to do something interesting with them. This recipe is made with what we had in the refrigerator, and it is so good. It is delicate, with layers of flavor and a touch of the unexpected, courtesy of the oyster emulsion.

Serves 4

For the oyster emulsion	6 fresh oysters bunch of Italian parsley juice of ½ lemon salt, to season
For the leeks	1 kg all-purpose (plain) flour, plus extra for dusting 300 g salt 500 ml water 2 sprigs thyme 2 leeks
For the orange curry	100 ml sunflower oil 200 g onion, brunoise 30 g garlic 40 g grated ginger 8 g ground cumin 8 g coriander seeds 5 g saffron 3 g smoked pepperoncini 600 ml Coconut Milk (see page 68) 300 g tamarind paste 85 g tomato paste (puree) 80 g peanut butter 250 ml water
For the thyme oil	80 ml sunflower oil 80 g thyme leaves 1 g grated cumari chile
To serve	3 green shiso leaves ½ green apple, sliced

Oyster emulsion Place the oysters and parsley in a blender and blend for 5 minutes. Add the lemon juice and salt. Refrigerate until needed.

Leeks Preheat the oven to 350°F (180°C). Grease a baking sheet and dust it with flour.

In a bowl, combine the flour, salt, and water. Knead for 5 minutes, or until the dough is smooth and no longer sticks to your hands. On a lightly floured surface, use a rolling pin to roll out the dough to a ¼-inch (5-mm) thickness. Place the thyme on top, then add the whole leeks. Fold the dough in half to seal and place it on the prepared baking sheet. Bake for 30 minutes. Remove from the oven, open the dough that surrounds the leeks, remove them, and cut in half lengthwise.

Place the leeks on a buttered baking sheet to heat for serving.

Orange curry Heat the oil in a skillet over medium heat. Add the onion and garlic and sauté for 3 minutes, or until browned. Add the ginger, cumin, coriander seeds, saffron, pepperoncini, coconut milk, tamarind paste, tomato paste (puree), and peanut butter. Bring to a boil and boil for 5 minutes. Add the water and cook for 30 minutes, or until reduced by half.

Transfer to a blender and blend for 3 minutes. Strain the mixture through a chinois.

Thyme oil Blend all the ingredients in a blender for 10 minutes, then strain.

To serve Arrange a leek on each plate. Top with orange curry, then the oyster emulsion, a drizzle of thyme oil, and the shiso leaves and apple slices.

Tuna, lard, and watermelon

My husband makes an excellent barbecue. Sunday is usually when he does the main courses, and I take care of the starters and side dishes. Sometimes when he is preparing the meat, I grill vegetables and fruits. Grilled (griddled) watermelon is one of my favorites. I knew I would make a dish like this one day. The moment came when I received a very good fatty tuna loin.

Serves 4

For the tuna	200 g fatty tuna loin 8 slices lard, each a 2½-inch (6-cm) square
For the watermelon	500 g watermelon 30 ml olive oil salt, to season
For the white sauce	400 g Brazil nuts 600 ml water 200 ml coconut water 50 ml emerina native bee honey salt, to season zest of 1 lemon
For the tucupi oil	100 g olive oil 30 g tucupi
To serve	cilantro (coriander), for garnish

Tuna	Cut the tuna loin into 4 pieces. Slice into ½- × 1½-inch (1- × 4-cm) sashimi. Arrange on a cheesecloth (muslin) at room temperature. Place a lard slice on each piece of tuna.
Watermelon	Preheat a grill to low (250°F/120°C). Cut the watermelon into ½- × 1½-inch (1- × 4-cm) slices, brush with the olive oil, and place on the grill. Grill for 40 seconds on each side.
White sauce	Place the Brazil nuts, water, coconut water, and honey in a Thermomix and mix for 12 minutes. Season with salt and lemon zest.
Tucupi oil	Combine the oil and tucupi in a small bowl and mix well.
To serve	Spread some sauce on each plate, arrange 3 slices of tuna with lard overtop, and then top with the grilled (griddled) watermelon slices. Drizzle with a little tucupi oil, then garnish with the cilantro (coriander).

Okra, black beans, and sea urchin

There was no fresh fish in Curitiba when I opened Manu, only frozen. I had to drive to the beach to buy fresh fish and shellfish. On one of those trips, I met Nininho, who lived in a special place in Paranaguá Bay, on Paraná's coast (page 100). He was a constant source of inspiration and watching him season beans with oysters inspired the idea of using seafood for seasoning the beans. The black bean sauce is the key to this dish. The other ingredients are important, but they are there for balance, texture, and deliciousness.

Serves 4

For the black beans	100 g black beans 2.4 L water 200 g mussels in the shell 20 g thyme leaves 1 bay leaf
For the sea urchin	8 sea urchins
For the okra	300 ml water 20 g sugar 4 okra 20 ml Cashew Nut Oil (see page 142) 10 ml rice vinegar 6 ml yuzu juice 2 g salt 2 g black pepper
For the crunchy bread (optional)	50 g sliced brioche 25 g clarified butter zest of 1 lime 1 g lemon thyme leaves salt, to season black pepper, to season
To serve	10 g purple oxalis sprouts

Black beans   Soak the beans in 400 ml of water for 4 hours. Drain.

In a large saucepan, combine the beans, mussels, thyme, and bay leaf. Add the remaining 2 L of water and cook over medium heat for 3 hours, or until the beans are tender (but not mushy) and cooked through. Strain the mixture through a chinois, pressing well to extract all the flavor.

Sea urchin   Open the sea urchin, take out the meat inside, and leave it in a bowl on ice.

Okra   In a saucepan, bring the water to a boil. Add a pinch of salt and the sugar. Add the okra and cook for 30 seconds. Transfer the okra to a bowl of ice water and set aside for 5 minutes. Pat dry, then slice into thick disks. Place in a bowl, and then season with cashew nut oil, vinegar, yuzu juice, salt, and pepper.

Crunchy bread Preheat the oven to 266°F (130°C).

Spread the brioche slices on a baking sheet and warm in the oven for 30 minutes, or until toasted. Transfer the toasted brioche to a food processor and process to a flour. Add the clarified butter, lime zest and lemon thyme leaves and blend on high speed until well mixed. Season with salt and pepper.

To serve   Heat the bean sauce in a saucepan over medium-low heat. Spread 150 ml of bean sauce on each plate. Add a spoonful of okra, and lay some crunchy brioche on top, if using. Arrange 2 pieces of sea urchin on each plate. Finish with the oxalis sprouts. Serve immediately.

Kefir, granola, and pollen

We use kefir as a fermentation starter at Manu, as my family has been doing since I was a toddler. I used it to compose this dessert that references the yogurt, honey, and granola that some people eat for breakfast. This recipe, though, combines pollen, honey, and a special granola.

Serves 4

For the granola
30 g licuri
25 g rice flakes
15 g brown sugar
12 g chia seeds
12 g quinoa
12 g flaxseeds
10 g corn flakes
35 ml honey

To serve
100 g kefir
100 g Yogurt Ice Cream
(see page 78)
50 g frozen borá stingless bee
pollen (needs to be frozen
to grate)
20 ml mandaçaia native bee honey

Granola   Preheat the oven to 250°F (120°C).

In a bowl, carefully mix all the ingredients together. Pour the mixture on a Silpat and bake for at least 20 minutes, stirring occasionally, until lightly browned. Remove from the oven and set aside to cool.

Transfer to an airtight container to preserve the crunchiness.

To serve   Lightly spread a spoonful of kefir on each plate. Place a spoonful of granola overtop, then a quenelle of yogurt ice cream. Using a microplane, grate the pollen over the ice cream. Drizzle a spoonful of mandaçaia native honey around the kefir.

Peanuts and sage

I love tasting all the herbs in the garden. My husband, Dario, is amazed that I know the name and uses of plants he would never notice. Sage is an herb I particularly like; it smells so good. The idea of pairing sage with peanut ice cream came to me one day when we were frying sage and I smelled the aroma of peanuts being prepared for another dish.

Serves 4

For the peanut butter	150 g roasted peanuts 30 g sugar
For the peanut ice cream	400 g regular unroasted peanuts 400 ml hot milk 150 g egg yolks 100 g sugar 300 g sour cream
For the dehydrated sage	1 g sage leaves
To serve	1 g ground coffee

Peanut butter   Place the peanuts and sugar in a blender and blend until smooth. Reserve 100 g of the peanut butter and store the rest for another use.

Peanut ice cream   Roast the peanuts well.

While still hot, transfer the peanuts to a Thermomix. Add the hot milk and mix for 2 minutes on high speed. Using cheesecloth (muslin), strain the liquid into a bowl. Save 300 g of this milk and store the rest for another use.

In the bowl of a stand mixer fitted with the whisk attachment, beat the yolks with the sugar until creamed and fluffy.

In a saucepan, heat the sour cream and peanut milk. Transfer the yolk mixture to a ceramic bowl and slowly whisk in the sour cream mixture. Cook in a bain-marie, stirring constantly, until it has a consistent, porridge-like texture. Let cool, then freeze.

Dehydrated sage   Dehydrate the sage leaves at 109°F (43°C) for 5 hours in a dehydrator.

To serve   To serve, add 100 g of peanut butter to the ice cream and gently mix.

Serve the ice cream in a bowl, overtop a sprinkling of ground coffee, with the sage leaves on top.

Strawberry and seaweed

Creating a seaweed dessert has always been a goal of mine. I like the sea air and the taste of it in desserts. Strawberries in season have a slight sweetness and acidity, perfect with the seaweed salsa.

Serves 4

For the seaweed salsa	10 g hydrated tapioca flour
	75 ml water
	10 g toasted nori sheets
	35 ml light soy sauce
	13 ml lemon juice

For the lemon oil	4 lemons
	120 ml sunflower oil

For the dill oil	100 g dill
	130 ml grapeseed oil

For the strawberry sorbet	230 g strawberries
	450 ml water
	105 ml honey

Seaweed salsa
In a small saucepan, combine the tapioca flour with 50 ml of water and cook over medium heat until it forms a gel. Remove from the heat and set aside. With scissors, chop the nori and place in a blender with the remaining 25 ml of water, soy sauce, and lemon juice. Blend on high speed until well combined. Add the tapioca gel and pulse to mix. Refrigerate until needed.

Lemon oil
Use a microplane to zest the lemons. Cut each lemon into 3 thick slices. Heat 10 ml of sunflower oil in a large heavy-bottomed skillet over high heat. Add the lemon slices and char both sides. Reduce the heat to medium heat and lightly press on the lemons to extract some of the juice. Using tongs, transfer the lemons to a plate lined with paper towel to drain well. Discard the lemon slices (or make a lemon bug for kombucha).

Reduce the heat to low, then add the remaining 110 ml oil to the skillet. Add the lemon zest and warm until fragrant, then remove immediately to prevent the zest from burning. Set aside at room temperature until needed.

Dill oil
Combine the dill and oil in a blender and blend for 3 minutes, or until the dill leaves are finely ground. Strain through a coffee filter with a weight on top for about 6 hours, until completely strained. Refrigerate until needed.

Strawberry sorbet
Combine all the ingredients in a pacotizing beaker. Seal and freeze at −8°F (−22°C) for at least 24 hours. Pacotize again before use.

To serve
Place a spoonful of seaweed salsa in each shallow bowl. Drizzle the lemon oil, along with a little lemon zest, into the bowls. Place a quenelle of strawberry sorbet in the center and finish with a drizzle of dill oil.

Chocolate and olive

Chocolate and extra-virgin olive oil are a perfect combination! So I thought, why not use it with olives as well? At first glance, it might seem like an odd combination, but it's fantastic. I'm a sweet-and-savory enthusiast, and this dessert is one of my long-time favorites.

Serves 4

For the olive and mint crumble	30 g mint leaves 50 g all-purpose (plain) flour 30 g cold butter 10 g sugar 200 g chopped dehydrated green olives
For the chocolate mousse	40 ml water 40 g superfine (caster) sugar 90 g egg yolks 160 g semisweet (dark) chocolate (70% cacao) 300 ml heavy (double) cream
To serve	15 ml extra-virgin olive oil 1 g fleur de sel

Olive and mint crumble   Preheat the oven to 250°F (120°C).

Wash and dry the mint leaves well. Cut them with scissors into small pieces.

In a bowl, combine the flour, cold butter, and sugar using your fingers, until it becomes a loose crumb. Add the mint and mix well. Place the mixture on a Silpat and dry in the oven for 30 minutes, taking care not to let it brown too much; otherwise it loses its color. Set aside to cool, then mix in the olives.

Chocolate mousse   Mix the water with the sugar in a small saucepan and bring to a boil over medium heat to make a syrup at a soft ball stage (241–244°F/116–118°C).

Meanwhile, beat the egg yolks in the bowl of a stand mixer fitted with the whisk attachment, until doubled in volume.

As soon as the syrup reaches the right temperature, pour in a stream over the yolks while beating on high speed, until doubled in volume.

Melt the chocolate in a bain-marie. Gently fold the melted chocolate into the yolk mixture. Stir in the cream.

To serve   Spoon mousse onto the plates. Top with the olive and mint crumble. Drizzle over the extra-virgin olive oil and sprinkle with a pinch of fleur de sel.

The Field to the Sea

Our home, our culture, our customs—there's a path that goes from the plateau to the coast, passing through mountains, valleys, and rivers. Nature around us brings us inspiration. These are our surroundings. We are part of this place. The place where our food comes from.

Shrimp tartare, vanilla, and coffee

My grandpa Nelson Buffara's parents came from Lebanon to Brazil to escape the Second World War, and I was raised eating a lot of Arab food. I love stuffed vine leaves, which in Brazil is also done with cabbage. Remembering the shrimp (prawns) my grandmother often served, I created this recipe with cabbage for the rolls and shrimp tartare to replace the meat that is traditionally used.

Serves 4

For the shrimp tartare	180 g fresh seven-beard shrimp 50 g pink salt 50 g sugar
For the shrimp sauce	2 kg Atlantic seabob shrimp (prawns) 1 stalk lemongrass 40 g ginger 1.5 L tucupi 700 g Brazil nuts ½ vanilla bean 15 g coffee beans salt, to season
For the roll	1 L water 4 cabbage leaves 100 ml rice vinegar 80 g sugar edible flowers, to decorate

Shrimp tartare Shell the shrimp (prawns), devein, and remove the heads. Combine the salt and sugar in a small bowl and rub over both sides of the shrimp. Place the shrimp on a wire rack set over a baking sheet and refrigerate for 1 hour to cure.

Rinse under running water, then chop the shrimp with the tip of a knife to make the tartare.

Shrimp sauce Remove the eyes from the shrimp. Place the whole unpeeled shrimp in a Thermomix and mix until a paste forms. Add the lemongrass and ginger and mix again to combine.

Transfer the mixture to a large saucepan and stir in the tucupi. Bring to a boil over medium heat, then stir again. Boil for 30 minutes. Strain the shrimp liquid.

In the Thermomix, combine the Brazil nuts, 1.4 L of shrimp liquid, vanilla bean, and coffee beans. Mix for 6 minutes, then strain into a bowl. Season with salt.

Roll In a saucepan, bring the water to a boil. Clean the cabbage leaves, removing the center stalk. Blanch the cabbage leaves in the boiling water for 1 minute. Drain, then cut the leaves in half lengthwise.

In a small saucepan, heat the vinegar and sugar over medium heat until syrupy.

To serve Mix a few spoonfuls of shrimp sauce with the tartare. Place the tartare on half a cabbage leaf and roll up like a cigar. Ladle sauce into each dish. Place the cabbage leaf in the center, brush with the syrup, and finish with the edible flowers.

Scallop and Brazil nut

I love scallops and always eat them when I'm by the sea, but they are so delicate that to serve them I have to be sure they are super fresh. When I found Paraíso das Ostras in the very southern part of Florianópolis, I felt safe preparing their scallops at the restaurant (page 108). They are super fresh and fleshy, and the exterior of the shells comes to me so clean that it would be possible to use them if we want to. The rest of the ingredients came together to enhance the scallops' freshness. The Brazil nut foam creates a puzzle, making the guests even more curious about what they are eating.

Serves 4

For the green sauce	200 g garlic chives
	60 g mint leaves
	15 g ground cumin
	50 g chives
	50 g cilantro (coriander) leaves
	50 g labneh
	100 g plain (natural) yogurt
	pinch of salt
For the cashew nut oil	1 kg cashew nuts
	1 L sunflower oil
For the Brazil nut foam	1 kg Brazil nuts
	2 L cold water
	60 ml lemon juice
	pinch of salt
	5 g gelatin sheet (hydrated in cold water)
For the fish roe sauce	50 g fish roe (sturgeon)
	80 ml coconut oil
For the uarini couscous	60 ml tucupi
	50 g uarini manioc flour
	10 g pimenta de cheiro (green chile pepper)
	15 g sliced scallion (spring onion)
	salt, to season
To serve	4 fresh scallops

Green sauce Pass the garlic chives through a juicer to extract the juice. Refrigerate the juice until cold.

Pour the juice into a blender, add the remaining ingredients, and blend at high speed for 5 minutes. Strain, then refrigerate until needed.

Cashew nut oil Combine the cashews and sunflower oil in a large saucepan and bring to a boil. Cook for 10 minutes at 300°F (150°C), or until the nuts are toasted. Remove from the heat, then cool the saucepan in an ice bath.

Transfer the mixture to a blender and blend at high speed for 10 minutes. Strain through cheesecloth (muslin), then store the cashew nut oil at room temperature until needed. (Leftover oil can be used in other recipes.)

Brazil nut foam Place the Brazil nuts and water in a large jar and cover with cheesecloth. Let stand at room temperature for 48 hours to ferment. Transfer the fermented mixture to a blender and blend at high speed for 10 minutes, or until smooth.

Pour the mixture into a saucepan. Warm over medium-low heat. Season with lemon juice and salt, then stir in the hydrated gelatin. Strain, then place in a siphon bottle and add 2 charges. Refrigerate for 6 hours.

Fish roe sauce Place the ingredients in a small bowl and blend using an immersion blender until emulsified. Transfer to a pipette and refrigerate until needed.

Uarini couscous Warm the tucupi in a small saucepan. Gradually add the uarini manioc flour, mixing continuously with a spoon. Add the chile and scallion (spring onion). Season with salt.

To serve Cut each scallop into 3 slices.

Put a drop of fish roe sauce in each bowl. Arrange the scallop slices in the bowl, then drizzle the cashew nut oil and green sauce around the scallops. Cover everything with the Brazil nut foam and finish with the uarini couscous. Serve immediately.

Baby corn, black garlic, and bottarga

Baby corn is pure charm. It has a sweet, delicate flavor and doesn't need fussy preparation. The black garlic enhances the delicate flavor and nuances of the corn, while the bottarga crumb brings an element of surprise to the dish. As well, both the bottarga and black garlic add umami.

Serves 4

For the black garlic salsa	15 g white miso paste
	10 g black garlic
	10 ml balsamic vinegar
	7 ml sunflower oil
	5 ml squid ink
	5 ml balsamic cream
	1 g lemon zest

| For the bottarga crumb | 100 g bottarga |
| | 25 g butter |

To serve	50 g labneh
	200 g baby corn
	20 ml olive oil
	fleur de sel, for sprinkling

Black garlic salsa   Put all the ingredients in a blender and blend well.

Bottarga crumb   Heat a skillet over high heat until hot. Add the bottarga and butter and brown for 5 minutes on each side. Reduce the temperature to 250°F (120°C) and break up the bottarga little by little, gradually drying it out, until crispy. Leave on low heat for at least 20 minutes, stirring constantly until completely dry.

Transfer the bottarga to a food processor and process until finely ground.

To serve   Lightly heat the black garlic salsa in a small saucepan over medium-low heat.

In a separate saucepan, lightly heat the labneh until it liquifies.

Heat a cast-iron skillet over medium-low heat. Cook the baby corns for 3 minutes on all sides until lightly charred. Add the olive oil and sauté quickly.

Place a little bit of black garlic salsa in the center of each plate. Arrange 3 baby corns on top. Drizzle a spoonful of liquid labneh over the black garlic salsa, forming a pattern. Cover the baby corn with the bottarga crumb and finish with fleur de sel.

Octopus, shiso, and avocado

I receive a lot of very good octopus at the restaurant, so I decided to make a reduction of it. We tried again and again until I finally discovered it went perfectly with lemon thyme and garlic. Since the protein went into the gel, I decided to make shiso leaf the centerpiece of the dish.

Serves 4

For the fish skin (optional)	100 g white fish skin, descaled, dehydrated at 100°F (37°C) for 12 hours pinch of salt
For the octopus reduction	1.5 kg octopus 25 ml rice vinegar 15 g lemon thyme 20 g garlic 20 g lemongrass 1.5 L water 100 g cassava starch
For the avocado sauce	2 ripe avocados juice of 1 lemon pinch of salt 1 garlic clove 100 ml olive oil
To serve	4 green shiso leaves, dehydrated at 100°F (37°C) for 3 hours

Fish skin	Cut the fish skin into little pieces and fry at 400°F (200°C) until it puffs and becomes crispy. Season with salt and store in an airtight container until needed.
Octopus reduction	In a stockpot, place the octopus, vinegar, lemon thyme, garlic, and lemongrass and cover with the water. Cook for 2 hours. Strain the stock into a medium stockpot. Let it reduce to half, then thicken with the cassava starch for 10 minutes, or until the texture becomes a gel.
Avocado sauce	With an immersion blender, blend together the avocados, lemon juice, salt, and garlic. Pour in the olive oil in a stream, continuing to blend until emulsified. Transfer to a pipette or pastry (piping) bag and let cool.
To serve	Place dots of avocado sauce and octopus reduction on each leaf and then 2 pieces of fish skin, if using. Serve immediately.

Tomatoes and acerola

Tomatoes are a national passion in Brazil. Whether alone, with oil, stuffed, or as a sauce, the tomato imparts a special flavor to dishes. Here I combine it with acerola, an acidic fruit that resembles the tomato and is super rich in vitamin C.

Serves 4

For the acerola salsa	250 g acerola fruit
	5 g chopped pimenta de cheiro (green chile pepper)
	7 g prunes
	15 g dried dates
	300 ml water
	125 ml tucupi
	10 ml vegetarian oyster sauce
	salt, to season
For the mint oil	100 g mint
	100 ml grapeseed oil
For the tomatoes	25 g Romanita tomato
	25 g sweet heart tomato
	25 g green cherry tomato
	25 g gold nugget tomato
	6 g raspberries
	6 g physalis
To serve	fleur de sel, for sprinkling
	lemon mint leaves
	dill
	micro basil leaves

Acerola salsa Cook the acerola in a skillet over medium heat, stirring occasionally, for 20 minutes, or until it breaks down. Add the chile and sauté. Add the prunes and dates and sauté for another 20 minutes. Add the water, tucupi, and oyster sauce and cook for 30 minutes. Strain the mixture through a chinois. Season with salt, then refrigerate until needed.

Mint oil Blanch the mint leaves in boiling water for 30 seconds. Transfer the leaves to a bowl of ice water and set them aside for 5 minutes. Drain, then dry them well with paper towel.

Spread the leaves on a tray and dehydrate at 95°F (35°C) for 8 hours.

In a blender, blend the dehydrated leaves and oil until smooth. Strain through a paper filter.

Tomatoes Cut all the tomatoes and raspberries in half. Thinly slice the physalis. Set aside until needed.

To serve Place 100 ml of acerola salsa in each deep dish. Arrange the tomatoes in one corner of the dish, cut side up. Arrange the raspberries and physalis around the tomatoes. Sprinkle the tomatoes with the fleur de sel. Finish with the herbs and a drizzle of mint oil.

Melon, peanuts, and coconut cheese

I am a huge fan of vegetables and try to create more dishes in which they play the most important role. And I love to bring fruits to the main courses. On top of that, this coconut cheese is fantastic.

Serves 4

For the coconut cheese	1 kg fresh coconut meat
	1 L whole (full–fat) milk
	100 g plain (natural) yogurt
	500 g salt
	1 L water
For the melon	1 x 300 g unpeeled Galia melon
For the peanut vinaigrette	100 g fresh unroasted peanuts
	150 ml water
	10 ml rice vinegar
	salt, to season
For the crisp	30 g chopped chives
	30 g chopped peanuts
	20 ml olive oil
	10 ml rice vinegar
	zest of 1 lemon

Coconut cheese Combine the coconut and milk in a saucepan over low heat and cook for 1½ hours without letting it boil. Remove the pan from the heat and let cool. Transfer the mixture to a blender and blend for 8 minutes, or until smooth. Strain the mixture through a chinois.

Return the strained milk to the pan, stir in the yogurt, and boil for about 9 minutes over low heat, until it curdles. Transfer to a bowl and refrigerate for 2 hours. Line a cheesemaker with a cheesecloth (muslin), pour in the curdled milk, and drain well. Transfer the cheesemaker to the refrigerator and leave for 48 hours. Remove from the refrigerator and remove the curd that formed on the cloth.

Combine the salt and water in a large bowl. Dip the curdled milk to the brine, then remove it. Remove the salt that formed on top of the curd. Leave the curd in an incubator at room temperature for approximately 6 days to ferment and mature the cheese.

Melon Peel the melon, starting about a ¼ inch (5 mm) from the base. Cut the melon into slices ¾-inch (2-cm) thick, place it on a wire rack set in a baking dish, and bake at 194°F (90°C) for 2 hours. Remove from the oven. Using a 1¼-inch (3-cm) circular ring, cut into circles and set aside.

Peanut vinaigrette Put all the ingredients in a blender and blend until emulsified.

Crisp Combine all the ingredients in a bowl and mix well.

To serve Arrange melon circles on each plate, then drizzle over the peanut vinaigrette. Grate or crumble the coconut cheese overtop and finish with the crisp.

Fish and green apple

There are two little details I like a lot in this recipe: the bee pollen added to the fish cure, and the zests of pink lemon in the apple cream. Pink lemon is an exceptional wild fruit that can only be found on farms and in backyards—we never see this kind of lemon in markets. But it transforms an otherwise ordinary fish cure and apple cream into something extraordinary.

Serves 4

For the fish	200 g yellowtail
	50 g sugar
	50 g salt
	30 g fresh Brazilian bee pollen, grated
	20 ml olive oil
	salt, to season
For the apple cream	40 ml rice vinegar
	30 g sugar
	2 green apples, unpeeled, chopped
	zest of 3 pink lemons
For the white cream	200 ml Coconut Milk (see page 68)
	80 g plain (natural) yogurt
	100 ml saiqui native bee honey
	70 g cubed cold butter
To serve	1 toasted (7- × 8-inch/ 18- × 20-cm) nori sheet

Fish Place the yellowtail fillets in a single layer on a wire rack set over a rimmed baking sheet. Combine the sugar and salt in a small bowl and rub over both sides of the fish. Cure in the refrigerator for 8 hours.

Cut the fish into ¼-inch (5-mm) cubes. Gently toss with the grated pollen, olive oil, and salt to season.

Apple cream Place the vinegar and sugar in a skillet over medium heat and boil until the vinegar has evaporated. Add the chopped unpeeled apples and lemon zest and cook for 40 minutes, stirring occasionally, until creamy. Transfer to a blender, blend until smooth, then strain. Refrigerate until needed.

White cream Place the coconut milk, yogurt, and honey in a blender and blend until combined. Pour the mixture into a saucepan and warm over medium heat to 212°F (100°C). Add the cubed butter, then use an immersion blender to emulsify.

To serve Crush the nori with your fingers, then pass it through a sieve to turn it into powder. Place some white cream at the bottom of the plates and arrange the fish in the center. Make a couple of circles of the apple cream around the fish, and finish with a sprinkling of nori powder overtop.

Oyster, palm heart, and bone marrow

This recipe was created after I met Nininho and Tati, a couple who lives on Ilha Rasa, a remote island near Paranaguá Bay (page 100). For four years, they were my suppliers of fish and wild fruits. They harvest very fresh oysters there, but they were taught by their parents to never eat them raw and they still don't. The oysters they prepare are amazing and rarely require seasoning.

Serves 4

For the coconut milk	200 g fresh grated coconut
	210 ml water
For the palm heart sauce	1 kg clean, fresh palm heart
	40 g chopped bacon
	20 g tapioca starch
	100 ml Coconut Milk (see above)
For the bone marrow	100 g bone marrow
	20 g finely chopped cilantro (coriander)
	20 g finely chopped mint
For the oysters	meat of 4 fresh oysters
	20 ml vegetable oil
For the charred herbs	2 g Italian parsley
	2 g dill

Coconut milk Put the coconut and water in a blender and blend for 5 minutes, or until smooth. (Because it is natural, it will not have the thickness or super white color of commercial coconut milk.) Strain the mixture into a bowl lined with a clean dish towel, squeezing well with your hands to extract all the milk.

Palm heart sauce Pass the palm heart through a juicer. In a saucepan, simmer the juice and the resulting pulp at 110°F (45°C) for 12 hours, until it ferments and reduces to 400 ml. Strain through a sieve and reserve. Fry the bacon in a skillet over medium heat. Add the fermented palm heart juice. Meanwhile, stir the starch into the coconut milk until dissolved. Let the palm heart sauce cook for 20 minutes, then add the starchy milk. Cook for 5 minutes, or until the mixture thickens. Keep warm until needed.

Bone marrow Cook the bone marrow in a skillet over medium heat until it melts. Add the herbs and keep the mixture warm until needed.

Oysters In a saucepan, heat the oyster meat in the vegetable oil until warmed through.

Charred herbs Place the herbs on a stainless-steel plate. Using a kitchen torch, char the herbs.

To serve Place the warm oysters on plates, cover with the warm palm heart sauce, and add a few drops of the bone marrow mixture on top and some charred herbs. Serve immediately.

Tuna, seafood, and orange

All my life experiences have reconnected me to the kitchen, which has always been present in my life. Even without realizing it, I've been influenced by my father, who came from the countryside, and by my mother, who came from the seaside. Tuna is one of the darling fishes of southern Brazil. We use bluefin when the Brazilian sea presents us with it, combining it with a mild salsa of clam, ginger, and lemongrass. I can sense my mother's beloved sea in this dish, but at the same time, with the orange, I reconnect to the countryside, where my father lives and works.

Serves 4

For the seafood salsa
50 g brown butter
    (beurre noisette)
150 g onion, brunoise
20 g grated ginger
20 g chopped lemongrass
300 g clam meat
150 ml dry white wine
600 ml Coconut Milk
    (see page 68)

For the orange
150 g Bahia orange (about 1)

For the tuna
300 g fresh tuna loin
fleur de sel, to season
extra-virgin olive oil, for drizzling

Seafood salsa Heat the brown butter (beurre noisette) in a skillet over medium heat. Add the onion and sauté for 20 minutes, or until golden. Add the ginger and lemongrass and sauté until they release their aroma. Increase the heat to medium-high, add the clams, and sauté until all the liquid has evaporated. Pour in the white wine and reduce the heat to low. Cook until the alcohol has evaporated.

Pour in the coconut milk, cover, and cook over low heat for 30 minutes. Transfer the hot mixture to a blender and blend on high speed for 5 minutes. Strain the mixture through a chinois.

Orange Segment the orange.

Tuna Cut the tuna into 4 pieces, about 1¼ × 2½ inches (3 × 6 cm).

To serve Place a piece of tuna in each deep dish and season with fleur de sel. Arrange orange segments over the tuna. Spoon 50 ml of the hot seafood salsa around the tuna and finish with a drizzle of extra-virgin olive oil.

This dish is one of those recipes everyone should eat at least once: the flavor is unique. The pâté reminds me of Christmas at my paternal grandmother's house. This is a more modern version, to be eaten with a spoon. Mixing the liver with vegetables intensifies its sweetness.

Serves 4

For the bok choy	250 g bok choy
For the orange salsa	350 ml orange juice 50 g brown butter (beurre noisette) 50 g cubed cold butter 2 g hydrated tapioca flour
For the curry salsa	10 ml sunflower oil 100 g onion, brunoise 15 g sliced garlic 20 g grated ginger 4 g ground cumin 4 g cilantro (coriander) with stems 2 g ground turmeric 1 g smoked pepperoncini 150 g tamarind paste 40 g peanut butter 40 g concentrated tomato puree 300 ml Coconut Milk (see page 68) salt, to season

For the peanut crunch	100 g chopped roasted peanuts
	50 g brown butter
	  (beurre noisette)
	5 g chopped pimenta de cheiro
	  (green chile pepper)
	salt, to season

To serve	10 g brown butter
	  (beurre noisette)
	100 g Chicken Liver Pâté
	  (see page 58)
	fleur de sel, for sprinkling

Bok choy Cut the bok choy in half lengthwise.

Orange salsa In a skillet, combine 150 ml of orange juice and the brown butter (beurre noisette) and bring to a boil over high heat. Boil for 8 minutes, or until the butter is caramelized and golden and the orange juice has caramelized. Add another 150 ml of orange juice to the skillet and bring to a boil. Add the cubed butter little by little, tilting the skillet to incorporate and emulsify it. Simmer on low heat until slightly thickened.

In a small bowl, stir the tapioca flour into the remaining 50 ml of orange juice until dissolved. Pour into the skillet and boil for 1 more minute, or until thickened.

Curry salsa Heat the oil in a skillet over medium heat. Add the onion and sauté until browned. Add the garlic and sauté until fragrant. Add the ginger, cumin, cilantro (coriander), turmeric, and pepperoncini and sauté for another 2 minutes, or until the aroma is released. Add the tamarind paste, peanut butter, and tomato puree and cook for 5 minutes, stirring constantly. Reduce the heat to low, pour in the coconut milk, and cook for 10 minutes. Season with salt. Transfer the hot mixture to a blender and blend for 10 minutes. Strain the mixture through a chinois.

Peanut crunch In a skillet, stir the peanuts with the butter and heat lightly over low heat. Add the chiles, then season with salt.

To serve Toast the bok choy on a grill, cut side down. Then fry them in brown butter (beurre noisette) in a hot skillet. Pour the orange salsa over the bok choy, making sure the sauce gets in between the leaves.

Place a spoonful of chicken liver pâté on each plate and top with the glazed bok choy. Spoon curry salsa between the bok choy leaves. Season with fleur de sel and top with the peanut crunch.

Lamb and beet

I like the light pink meat and delicate flavor of the Hampshire Down lamb breed we buy from a local producer. It matches the color of beet (beetroot) so well that I decided to use them together. I use the whole lamb carcass, and use beet juice instead of wine to make the glace.

Serves 4

For the demi-glace Part 1	4 kg osso buco
	4 kg oxtail
	1 kg pig feet
	50 ml cognac
	750 ml dry red wine
	12 L water
	5 g black peppercorns
Part 2	1.2 kg white (button) mushrooms
For the glazed beets	100 g small beets (beetroot)
	100 ml beet (beetroot) juice
	50 ml cranberry juice
	30 ml light soy sauce
	5 g ground cumin
	25 g cubed cold butter
For the beef and beet salsa	80 ml Demi-Glace (see above)
	25 ml reserved Glazed Beets sauce (see above)
For the lamb	1 g fine pink salt
	1 g sugar
	180 g lamb T-bone steak, without bone (about 1 loin)
	olive oil, for brushing
	20 g butter
To serve	fleur de sel, for sprinkling

Demi-glace Part 1 Preheat the oven to 350°F (180°C). Place the osso buco, oxtail, and pig feet in a roasting pan and bake for 1 hour, turning the pieces halfway through.

Transfer the osso buco and oxtail to a stockpot, reserving the pig feet for the glaze. Add the cognac and red wine and reduce over medium heat by half.

Meanwhile, cold-smoke the pig feet for 20 minutes to coax out the flavor. Place the roasting pan over medium heat, pour in 1 L of water, and deglaze, scraping the bottom of the pan with a spoon.

Once the wine has been reduced in the pot, add the pig feet and 6 L of water.

In a heavy-bottomed skillet, toast the black peppercorns until fragrant. Add the peppercorns to the stock and gently simmer the stock for 36 hours. Pour in the remaining 5 L of water and reduce over low heat for another 36 hours. You should have 3 L of stock.

Strain the stock into a bowl. Refrigerate for at least 12 hours to separate the solid fat from the stock. Skim off this layer of fat and discard.

Part 2 Bring the demi-glace to a boil in a stockpot.

Meanwhile, heat a heavy-bottomed skillet over medium heat. Arrange the mushrooms in the skillet with the stems up and toast well. Transfer the mushrooms to a bowl, cover immediately, and set aside for 30 minutes, for the mushrooms to release their liquid.

Add the mushrooms to the stock and cook over low heat for 1½ hours, until reduced by half. Strain the demi-glace through a chinois. Set aside.

Glazed beets Preheat the oven to 350°F (180°C). Wrap each beet (beetroot) in aluminum foil and bake for 30–50 minutes, until tender. Remove the beets from the oven and let cool. Peel the beets, then cut them in half.

In a skillet, bring half of the beet juice, the cranberry juice, soy sauce, and cumin to a boil. Boil until reduced by a third. Add half of the cold butter, tilting the skillet to incorporate and emulsify it, until the mixture has thickened. Add the rest of the beet juice and the remaining butter, alternating them. Stir until well blended. Reserve 25 ml of this sauce to make the beef and beet salsa. Reserve the beets in the skillet until needed.

Beef and beet salsa Combine the demi-glace and glazed beets sauce in a saucepan and cook over medium heat for 30 minutes, or until reduced by half. Set aside until needed.

Lamb In a small bowl, combine the salt and sugar. Rub over the lamb, then place the lamb on a wire rack set over a baking sheet to cure, uncovered in the refrigerator, for 4 hours. Pat dry the lamb with paper towel.

Heat a skillet over high heat. Brush the lamb with a little olive oil and sear on each side for 30 seconds. Add the butter to the skillet and cook the lamb for another 30 seconds on each side. Transfer to a wire rack to rest for 4 minutes.

To serve Heat the beets with their sauce over medium heat, taking care not to scorch them. (If the sauce starts to curdle, emulsify again with a little beet juice.) Warm the beef and beet salsa.

Cut the lamb into 4 pieces and arrange one on each plate, cut side up. Place a beet half beside each piece of lamb, along with a little beet sauce. Cover one end of the lamb loin with 1 tablespoon of salsa and finish with the fleur de sel. Serve immediately.

Milk, yogurt, and chocolate

I love bringing new ingredients to the restaurant kitchen. I fell in love with the smell of priprioca, but I couldn't find a recipe for this Amazonian root. It has a unique flavor and aroma and is widely used in perfumes but not as widely in cooking. Indigenous people use it a lot for seasoning.

One afternoon, Vanessa Lima, Manu's pastry chef, was making ambrosia (a kind of salted caramel), and I suggested adding priprioca. It was almost perfect but ultimately too sweet. I love passion fruit, and its powder adds a certain delicacy to the yogurt foam while breaking the sweetness of the priprioca ambrosia.

Serves 4

For the priprioca ambrosia
1 L whole (full-fat) milk
160 g sugar
15 g egg yolks
105 g egg whites
50 ml lime juice
50 g grated priprioca root

For the yogurt foam
2 gelatin sheets
30 ml cold water
500 g plain (natural) yogurt
25 ml lime juice
20 ml mandaçaia native bee honey

For the passion fruit powder
150 g sour passion fruit pulp

For the white chocolate mousse
75 g white chocolate
165 g egg whites
100 g sugar
22 g egg yolks
75 g powdered milk

Priprioca ambrosia Combine the milk and the sugar in a heavy-bottomed saucepan and bring to a boil over medium heat. Boil for 10 minutes.

Meanwhile, sieve all the yolks and whisk with the egg whites. Add the egg mixture little by little to the hot milk, whisking continously to prevent the eggs from cooking. And the lime juice and grated priprioca. Cook on low heat, stirring occasionally, for 1–2 hours, until the liquid has evaporated and the ambrosia is slightly brown. Let cool, then refrigerate until needed.

Yogurt foam Soak the gelatin sheets in the cold water for 1 minute, then drain (it will not be completely dissolved). Combine the gelatin and yogurt in a saucepan and cook over medium heat (do not exceed 140°F/60°C) until the gelatin dissolves. Remove the pan from the heat, then stir in the lime juice and honey. Strain the mixture through a chinois, then pour into a 0.5-L siphon. Load the siphon with 2 charges and refrigerate for at least 4 hours.

Passion fruit powder Spread the passion fruit pulp on a Silpat and dehydrate for 24 hours at 100°F (37°C). Transfer to a blender and blend to a powder. Store in an airtight container until needed.

White chocolate mousse Preheat the oven to 212°F (100°C).

Melt the white chocolate in a bain-marie. Meanwhile, with a hand mixer on high speed, beat together the egg whites and sugar until peaks form. Add the egg yolks. Reduce the speed and gradually add the melted chocolate and powdered milk, alternating them. Mix until incorporated.

Spread the mixture on a Silpat and bake for 1 hour. Let cool. Coarsely chop the dehydrated mousse sheets, then store them in an airtight container until needed.

To serve Spread a spoonful of ambrosia on each plate. Cover it with the yogurt foam, sprinkle with passion fruit powder, and add 2 or 3 pieces of the coarsely chopped dehydrated mousse.

Kiwi, yogurt, cilantro, and popcorn

Sometimes I like to play with colors. This dish has a variety of greens—from kiwi, green apple, and cilantro (coriander). The yogurt foam and the popcorn balance each other and give movement and grace to the dish.

Serves 4

For the kiwi sorbet	160 g sugar
	120 ml water
	300 g kiwis
	200 g green apple (about 1)
	½ lime
	240 g unpeeled cucumber

For the green sauce	738 g sorrel leaves
	248 g cilantro (coriander)
	200 ml tucupi
	100 g cashew nuts
	100 g Boursin cheese
	50 ml olive oil

For the sweet popcorn	200 g sugar
	240 ml hot water
	120 ml coconut oil
	200 g popcorn kernels

For the yogurt foam	500 g plain (natural) yogurt
	120 g quark cheese
	100 g confectioners' (icing) sugar
	80 ml whole (full-fat) milk
	50 ml heavy (double) cream

Kiwi sorbet Combine the sugar and water in a saucepan and warm over high heat until the mixture reaches 244°F (118°C). Remove from the heat and let cool.

Peel the kiwis and cut each into 4 pieces. Dehydrate at 113°F (45°C) for 10 hours. Cut the apple in half, remove the seeds and squeeze the lime over the exposed apple flesh. In a juicer, extract the juice from the apple and then from the cucumber. Add the kiwis to the juice, then transfer to a blender and blend well. Strain, then mix with 60 g of sugar syrup. Put it in the freezer.

Green sauce Combine all the ingredients in a blender and blend for 6 minutes. Reserve.

Sweet popcorn Heat the sugar in a deep skillet over medium heat, stirring occasionally, until dissolved and golden. Add the hot water and stir carefully. Add the oil and mix well.

Reduce the heat to low and add the popcorn kernels. Stir for 1 minute, then cover with a lid. Upon hearing the first pop, increase the heat to high and keep covered until the popcorn stops popping. Let cool, then transfer to a blender and blend to a powder. Reserve.

Yogurt foam Combine all the ingredients in a bowl, stirring to mix well. Place in a siphon and load 2 charges. Refrigerate for at least 8 hours.

To serve Put 4 teaspoons of the green sauce in each bowl, then top with kiwi sorbet. Top the sorbet with the yogurt foam and finish with the popcorn powder.

Strawberry, mullet roe, and lemon

I am a massive fan of mullet roe, and I find it is very versatile. When I cook in Europe, I serve a dessert with caviar. Since we do not have caviar in Brazil, I decided to instead use mullet roe, which we process to a powder. It also goes well with the oil we make with lemon. I love this dessert!

Serves 4

For the strawberry	200 g strawberries
For the crunchy coconut	70 g fresh grated coconut
	80 g all-purpose (plain) flour
	40 g sugar
	60 g butter
	0.5 g grated amburana
For the mullet roe	5 g salt, plus extra to season
	5 g sugar
	1 x 200 g piece mullet roe
	20 g butter
	zest of 1 lemon
For the lemon oil	4 lemons
	120 ml sunflower oil
To serve	4 quenelles Yogurt Ice Cream (see page 78)

Strawberry With an immersion blender, blend the strawberries until smooth. Refrigerate until needed.

Crunchy coconut Preheat the oven to 300°F (150°C).

Spread the grated coconut on a Silpat. Bake for 6–8 minutes, stirring occasionally, until it is dry and crunchy. Remove from the oven and let cool. Increase the oven temperature to 347°F (175°C).

In a bowl, combine the coconut, flour, sugar and the butter and mix until it becomes a loose crumb. Add the grated amburana and mix well. Place the mixture on a Silpat and bake for 30 minutes, or until dry and crunchy. Remove from the oven and let cool. To maintain its crunch, store in an airtight container until needed.

Mullet roe Combine the salt and sugar in a small bowl. Sprinkle the cure over the roe. Place the roe on a wire rack set over a baking sheet and refrigerate at 41°F (5°C) for 3 days, until dried and cured. Peel off and discard the thin top layer of the roe, then coarsely chop.

Heat a heavy-bottomed nonstick skillet over medium heat. Combine the butter and roe and braise well, stirring continuously, until the roe is crunchy. Season with salt and the lemon zest. Remove from the heat and let cool. Put the mixture in a blender and blend to a fine powder.

Lemon oil Use a microplane to zest the lemons and set aside. Cut each lemon into 3 thick slices. Heat 10 ml of sunflower oil in a large heavy-bottomed skillet over high heat. Add the lemon slices and char both sides. Reduce the heat to medium and lightly press on the lemons to extract some of the juice. Using a skimmer, transfer the lemons to a plate lined with paper towel to drain well.

Reduce the heat to low, then add the remaining 110 ml of oil to the skillet. Add the lemon zest and warm until fragrant, then remove immediately to prevent the zest from burning. Set aside at room temperature until needed.

To serve Put 2 tablespoons of strawberry puree in each bowl. Place some crunchy coconut in the center of the puree. Put a quenelle of yogurt ice cream on the coconut. Put the roe powder in a 1-tablespoon measure and then hold a lighter beneath the spoon to slightly warm it. Top the ice cream with the roe. Drizzle 1 teaspoon of lemon oil over the strawberry puree and serve.

Brazil nut popsicle
(or popsicle 1.0)

I have special affection for this recipe. In the south of Brazil, we like to drink yerba mate, and I am also a huge fan of nut milk. At the restaurant, it took a while for us to develop this delicious Brazil nut milk, but we discovered that when the nuts are toasted, the resulting flavor is much better. Since we had the milk, we decided to make a popsicle, something we always eat at the beach. When I tried it, I closed my eyes and waited for the missing flavor to come. Yerba mate was the answer.

Serves 4

For the Brazil nut milk	300 g toasted Brazil nuts 450 ml whole (full-fat) milk
For the Brazil nut popsicle	90 g egg yolks (about 5) 100 g sugar 300 ml heavy (double) cream 300 ml Brazil Nut Milk (see above)
For the chocolate glaze	220 g semisweet (dark) chocolate (77% cacao) 120 ml coconut oil
To serve	fleur de sel, for sprinkling 30 g yerba mate powder

Brazil nut milk — Heat a skillet over medium-high heat. Add the Brazil nuts and toast for 7–9 minutes, stirring frequently to prevent them from burning. Transfer to a blender, pour in the milk, and blend on high speed for 10 minutes. Strain the mixture through a chinois, extracting all the liquid, and reserve.

Brazil nut popsicle — In the bowl of a stand mixer fitted with the whisk attachment, mix the egg yolks and sugar on high speed until very pale.

Meanwhile, combine the cream and Brazil nut milk in a saucepan and heat over medium heat until warmed through. Gradually mix the heated cream into the yolk mixture, stirring lightly to incorporate. Place the mixture in a warm water bath for 10 minutes—do not let the temperature exceed 140°F (60°C). Remove from the heat and let cool completely. Pour into silicone popsicle molds. Freeze for at least 6 hours.

Chocolate glaze — Melt the dark chocolate with the coconut oil in a water bath until homogenous. Do not let the temperature exceed 122°F (50°C). Remove from the bath and let cool to 95°F (35°C).

To serve — Remove the popsicles from the molds and dip them in the chocolate glaze (at 95°F/35°C). Place them on parchment paper and sprinkle with the fleur de sel. Freeze them for 10 minutes.

Remove the popsicles from the freezer and dust with yerba mate powder. Serve immediately.

Passion Fruit

Brazil is the world's largest producer and consumer of fresh passion fruit, which comes from a family of hundreds of species, most of them native to South and Central America.

Curitiba, artisanal fishing, and fine dining

Leading up to hosting the 2014 World Cup and the 2016 Olympics, Brazil was the place everyone wanted to be. And Brazilian food and ingredients were something to experience. After four years of working as a food manager at Deville hotels, I decided to start my own business, in 2011. Back then, Curitiba had good international restaurants, including traditional ones with strong Italian and German influences thanks to their immigrant owners. Small dishes using local ingredients were featured in the food sections of magazines, though these were certainly not something to be served at a restaurant.

There was only one place in Curitiba to get a chef's degree: Centro Europeu (where I had attended). But the local chefs were skeptical of having interns working in their kitchens.

I had traveled, studied in Italy, and visited villages much smaller than Curitiba, where Michelin-starred chefs had succeeded. I knew Curitiba was big enough, and—even more importantly—had quality ingredients, and my restaurant project could work. I also knew that I would need to work hard.

According to Curitiba's Tourism Department, the city had 375 restaurants in 2012, and none of them was under the "contemporary kitchen" label. It took a while for people to hear of me, that's true. But I did not give up. I faced many challenges in the early days. For instance, only frozen fish was available in Curitiba at that time. So I had to travel to the seaside to buy fresh fish and shellfish. I started long conversations with Bernardo from Trapiche Pescados to persuade him to look for artisan fish suppliers to bring me fresh products. Today, he is one of my best suppliers.

Ten years passed, and the number of Curitiba's restaurants multiplied by three. Besides Centro Europeu, the city has at least ten good culinary schools and gastronomy courses—at PUC-PR, Senac, and Positivo. The only branch of the San Francisco Baking Institute, founded by boulanger Michel Suas, opened a few blocks from Manu. Many chefs are now offering fine-dining and tasting menus; everyone wants to be labeled a contemporary restaurant on the "best restaurants" lists. Trapiche Pescados became Curitiba's most important fish supplier, providing fresh amberjack, common snook, yellowfin, squids, crabs, crayfish, and a large variety of shrimp (prawn). It also offers an excellent mullet roe, well regarded by many of Curitiba's chefs.

From my little open kitchen, I sowed ideas, techniques, concepts, and ingredients for the city. I also brought my courage and my faith in a more sustainable world, where people would eat what is grown next to them, where they would learn to recognize edible mushrooms and seaweed happened upon during weekends hiking or scuba diving. I helped create eco-gastronomy and family agro-industry projects, and gave artisanal and sustainable fishing visibility.

I helped create projects to strengthen gastronomy in Curitiba, saw the non-profit organization Sebrae aid small farmers and producers, supported national festivals like Prazeres da Mesa (Pleasures of the Table), and took part in urban farms and zero-food-waste projects.

I do not consider it an exaggeration to say that Chef Alex Atala put Brazil on the world gastronomic map. When he and writer and food curator Andrea Petrini said I did the same for Curitiba, it put a smile on my face. To be clear: it's teamwork, but my fingerprints are there.

Creativity, cadence, and new possibilities

In 2016, fruits and vegetables became an important aspect of the restaurant. This year also happened to be the year I embraced the Urban Farms project, in which chefs lead workshops, teaching better ways of using the vegetables cultivated by Curitiba communities in poor areas. I also started a more sentimental phase of my work, using fewer ingredients and ensuring each of them had a purpose in the dish. My second daughter, Maria, was born a year and a half after Helena. I would take the girls with me on each visit to the Urban Farms project; I like to teach them where the food they eat comes from. I remember feeling so much joy upon seeing Helena pull a strawberry from the soil, clean it with her little hands, and eat it.

I started cooking and teaching at workshops, in Brazil at first. Before long, I was invited to do the same abroad. My trips became so frequent that we had a map in my children's bedroom so I could show them where I was going. To say goodbye, instead of telling them I was working abroad, I would say, "I'm going to change the world."

In 2019, my creativity reached new heights. I felt freer than ever before and took greater risks in flavor combinations. I was also even more in love with vegetables. When the pandemic put the world on pause, my schedule was full. Looking back, 2020 was a year of rescuing. I spent more time with my daughters, listened to my favorite songs again, and cooked at home a lot for the family. This was when I formed the group *Mulheres do Bem* (Women That Do Good), a team of chefs who cook once a week for the homeless. I also created the Manu Buffara Institute, to better organize and promote my community projects.

I opened Manuzita, a pop-up sandwich shop outside Manu. The sandwiches were prepared with house-made brioche and chicken, crab, roast beef, lentils, and many other options, along with unique sauces and crunchy greens. There was always a drink, including wine, to pair with them. During this time, Ella, my restaurant project in New York City, also took form. Ella allows me to showcase with a Brazilian flair the colorful dishes I serve to my friends and family at home.

The quality in a Paraíso das Ostras scallop is in a clean shell and vibrantly colored meat.

Time, motivation, and enthusiasm

We are all born capable of creating. And the key to producing plays, books, or recipes is to ensure a fertile ground for these ideas to flourish, grow, and bear flowers and fruits. Ever since I awoke my passion for cooking, I worked on developing the conditions needed for my ideas to take shape. My approach is slightly crazy—opening space for things to come up, and testing. I am constantly creating.

My sous-chef Lucas Correia and the cook Henrique Lorkievicz, who watch me invent all the time, joke that I was a saucier in a past life. According to them, all my dishes start by developing a sauce. Then I decide on the vegetable or protein to pair with it. Next, I develop textures and other dish details. Admittedly, they do have a point—I frequently work in that manner, but that isn't always the case, even though all my dishes have at least one very good sauce.

When I need to release a new menu, I dedicate more time to creative exercises. Time, motivation, and enthusiasm are also essential for inventing dishes. I start by cataloging the ingredients according to the season I intend to serve the dishes. I believe in an intuitive form of creativity that requires observing the elements. Each ingredient has its cooking time and its characteristics. I spend hours at the market, looking at the vegetables. I talk to gardeners at the urban gardens and fishers at the docks. I'm continuously having conversations about the wind, the rain levels of the season, the types of harvested vegetables, and the shellfish catches on the fishing boats and whether they are fat or sweet. Then I draft a long list of fresh ingredients that could appear in the recipes. I affix this list to the wall in my office, carrying a copy everywhere I go. Long-haul flights are my favorite times to stare at this list and let my mind make connections. After a couple of weeks of doing this exercise, ideas form. Sometimes they come in dreams. Sometimes the starting point is a sauce, while other times it is an uncommon pairing like passion fruit and cauliflower (page 111), strawberry and bottarga, shiso and octopus. And my notebook is always nearby, so I can write down my ideas.

My team gets a little agitated when I am in the midst of one of those processes. My sous-chef Debora Teixeira warns everyone to pay attention to what I am doing. And she has good reason. When looking for a flavor, I do not measure anything. Like a cartoon alchemist, I will mix herbs, vegetables, and bones in my cauldron. I open the restaurant's refrigerator to find an old cassava fermentation or buttermilk, and take tomatoes from the staff's food. Sometimes, I end up with a recipe virtually impossible to reproduce. Then the gang has to rack their brains trying to recreate the flavor. It took more than three months for us to recreate the squid ink sauce I made in one of those creative moments.

At this stage, I am even more committed to the kitchen than usual. You must look beyond the product before you, and go beyond the conventional. When everyone goes one way about an ingredient in my hands, I go the opposite direction. I keep this concept at the back of my mind—this is evident when you see some of our desserts at Manu. There is a melon ice cream with lard (page 82) inspired by the Parma ham and melon I ate at my mother's house. Parma ham comes from a pig and lard does as well. I did the same with mullet roe and strawberry. I love the acidity of strawberries, and when cooking abroad, I often blend caviar with them. Since we do not have caviar in Brazil but delicious mullet roe, I developed a dessert recipe combining them (page 166). My dessert chef, Vanessa, follows a traditional school of baking, executing recipes to perfection and always bringing me what I want. But I am the one to propose unusual processes and mixing flavors. Together, we make a nice duo.

Most times, recipes do not come together immediately. Many flavors I developed were shelved for months before being used. For instance, the sourdough sauce that gives soul to the carrot recipe (page 74) was made almost a year before we paired it with carrot. It has a strong acidity and greasiness that is hard to combine with seafood and other ingredients. But I knew that, in time, another ingredient or preparation would come along that would pair well with it. And when I perfected the cook point for the carrot a year later, I asked the team to bring me the sourdough sauce and the magic happened.

I also like to consider the feelings I want to arouse with a plate of food. I do not make food just for people to be happy. Sometimes I want to take my guests on a journey to the farm the ingredient came from. I do this with my meat dishes, which tend to have shades of brown, reminiscent of the land the pigs and lambs came from. And I always mix them with greens, a nod to the grass that fed the animals. All my fish plates, on the other hand, are bright. In my mind, they are connected to summer, and to the white sand of the beaches.

There is also a sense of painting in the assembly of a plate. Yes, I look for the harmony of colors, but I want to provoke reactions even before the diner lifts the food to their mouth. I care about the design of each dish that leaves the kitchen. I believe we start eating with our eyes. My sous-chef Lucas Correia, with whom I always have clever conversations about ingredients, says that he always anticipates a phone call from abroad when I'm cooking somewhere else: I may have caught sight of a photo posted on Instagram by a customer who mentioned my name and complained that the flowers were in the wrong place in this or that dish. It's possible for me to be present in the kitchen, even when I'm miles away.

I've learned a lot by listening. Since day one at Manu, our butter has been homemade. The first butter I ever made was from a recipe from Elaine, who works at my father's farm. She takes milk from a cow, leaves it in the milk canister, and waits for the cream to form on the surface. She then separates the cream, leaving it at room temperature for twenty-four hours. The next day, using a stand mixer or by hand, she fervently beats the cream and removes the whey in a process called "washing the butter." I'd prepared the restaurant's butter this way for some years when a friend told me how her mother used cream and yogurt to make butter. I was intrigued by the potential and have since discovered many ways to make butter with yogurt. I eventually developed a recipe that I use today (page 116). We use the cream and yogurt to make Manu's restaurant butter. And instead of letting the cream sit for twenty-four hours, we leave it for forty-eight hours, so the fermentation goes further.

Our yogurt is also made in-house, with "MC kefinho" (little kefir), the nickname being the team's reference to the emcees of the rap world. Like those who introduce the sounds at rap shows, our kefir introduces a lot to our preparations. I make the kefir the same way my grandmother did when I was a child. Having grown up listening to the cooks at my parents' and grandparents' homes, I've created a rich coconut milk also. I have to restrain myself from drinking a glass of coconut milk every time it's ready. It smells *so good*. With this coconut milk, we make a nice yogurt that's used in several dishes. A third starter we always have in the kitchen is the ginger bug, a fermentation made with ginger, water, and sugar.

I have always believed in my work, my potential, and the ingredients. Transforming the simple is much more difficult than using a truffle, for instance, which is impressive even on a fried egg. Using Brazilian products and understanding my ancestry, culture, and family are all part of my "authorial" voice. It took time and needed a pinch of maturity, but once I assumed my identity, I was able to tell stories through my menus. And each year, I enjoy creating these stories from the best my land, and my people, have to offer.

White onions, yellow onions, red onions, and shallot

I have an attachment to every ingredient used in my kitchen. Everyone makes a fuss when invited to taste wine, beer, foie gras, and chocolate, but I think that same enthusiasm should be expressed when trying garlic, coriander, asparagus, and greens.

One day when I arrived at the restaurant kitchen, I noticed that a cook had substituted the yellow fried onion we use in a shrimp (prawn) recipe with shallot. "It looks so much better," he added. I took a long breath. Then I asked him to bring all the onions he could find in the kitchen. He returned with white onions, big and mini yellow onions, big and mini red onions, sweet onions, scallions (spring onions), and his charming shallot. I asked him to soak, fry, bake, and grill each of them. I also asked him to plate each. The cook and I tried all the onions together. People rarely take the time to do this, but this kind of exercise happens regularly in Manu's kitchen. Even onions have a perfect temperature and texture when it comes to preparation. There is a pinnacle of flavor and texture for every ingredient—and any kind of onion. Over-fry an onion and it becomes bitter. And it must be added to the plate at the final moment before serving; otherwise, it will be less crispy. A good cook cares about these simple details when preparing each dish.

When a recipe calls for onion, you likely use whatever is available in your kitchen. And usually, it's the standard yellow variety, which is the cheapest option at the market. The "right" onion adds depth of flavor to a dish, which is something I look for. Yellow onions are the best bet if the recipe does not specify a type. They last longer, and, when fresh, they bring you to tears the moment your knife pierces the skin. They are spicy, pungent, and challenging to eat raw, so I use them in lengthy preparations, demi-glaces, stocks, sauces, and soups. But when it comes to sautés, I love to use white onions, which are harder to find and don't make you cry as much. They are crispy, watery, and pleasant to eat raw because of their sweetness.

Red onions, which are, in fact, purple, are best for raw preparations, as they are tasty and easy to caramelize because of their high sugar content. They go well in sandwiches, salads, and salsas. Sweet onions are usually larger than the other onions, and they do not last long. This thin-skinned variety is very sweet, and I know people who eat them like apples. They have little complexity and do not suit long cooking times, but they are the best for onion rings and are delicious on grills and raw salads. Shallots, mild and subtle in flavor, are suitable for vinaigrettes, omelets, and mushroom sauces.

After tasting each vegetable in its different preparations, the cook said he never thought onions could differ so much and realized now that the sweetness of the yellow onion indeed did work best with the shrimp. The bitterness of the fried shallot could spoil the dish.

Routine, checklists, and resilience

I am an obsessive organizer. I sort the clothes in my closet by color and length, and I can tell instantly if even a pair of socks has been moved out of place. I know the power of routine. And my sous-chef Debora Teixeira does as well. We have developed our best practices and we stick to them. We have lists we check every morning before starting service. We double-check that all the ingredients for each step of the menu are ready for the mise en place, and whether the yeast is suitable for making sourdough. We write down the name of the fish of the day and whether it will be served raw or cooked. If we host an event, all the details go on the checklist. If I'm traveling, the ingredients I have to pack will be listed. It is repetitive, but it is better to make a run for thyme at 11 a.m. than to discover in the middle of service that you're out of it and cannot prepare one of the main sauces on the menu.

Before each service, we have a meeting where everyone on the team is informed about the patrons that night, any dietary restrictions, if they are visiting for a special occasion, and if they are regulars or first-timers. We also have a checklist to close the restaurant and weekly checklists that change for each tasting menu. For example, for The Field to the Sea menu (page 139), Wednesday was the day we hydrated the uarini manioc flour (made from cassava) used on Saturday for the scallop recipe (page 142)—this was recorded on the list. This way, the dish's levels of complexity grew by the day.

The routines are not only in checklists—we are exacting in our measurements. Every ingredient is weighed before any preparation. We know for how long a 120-gram or a 200-gram carrot should remain in the oven. And I am strict when it comes to clean equipment and kitchen; cleanup cannot wait until tomorrow. I also visit each table by the end of service and say, "Thank you for choosing Manu tonight." I mean it. I feel honored for it to be chosen from so many options in the city.

Greatness is achieved through repetition, and perfection results from a good routine. And routine also presupposes training. Before we put together a menu, I thoroughly test each dish. Training also includes how to plate, how to serve the meal, and what to say to customers about the dish. I have a rule for the front-of-house team: every time a guest leaves the table, a clean and ironed napkin will be waiting for them upon their return. When I opened the restaurant, I used tablecloths (page 89). They are no longer used, but I kept the napkins. It is part of the waiters' daily routine to iron and fold them. I make no concessions when it comes to the napkins!

I received massive criticism when I opened a tasting menu only restaurant in Curitiba that did not serve risotto and fillet steak (page 89). People didn't think I'd survive the first year. Manu has been at the same address in the Batel neighborhood for over a decade now, and life is getting better. Ease comes from confidence and assurance that can only be nurtured over time; it comes with experience. I've been faithful to myself and my purpose: I had a dream, knew what I wanted, and gave my best. There were hard days. Monday and Tuesday nights would pass with very few diners, but I kept my dream going by closing the restaurant on those days. I spread my message, and people started to come. These days, we're fully booked for most dinners. And I am proud to say that I never bent to anyone, nor did anything I didn't believe in. It has made all the difference.

Helena, Maria, and Snow

It's a Thursday morning in late January and I'm sitting at my kitchen table with my daughters, Helena and Maria, aged seven and five respectively. If I look to the right, I can see my gas stove and the light that comes through two latticed windows over the big sink. A little closer is a sizeable rectangular countertop where several people can work comfortably side by side, while three others can watch them from the other side, sitting on high stools. To the left is our merle border collie, Snow, sitting outside by the glass sliding door leading to the barbecue and swimming pool area.

I just had some coffee, and the girls are having fresh coconut water and French toast I prepared with leftover brioche from Manu. I love when they say I make the best French toast they've ever had. My secret is to blend the eggs using a stand mixer until emulsified, then add a few drops of vanilla extract, cinnamon, a pinch of salt, a little panettone mix, and milk. I soak the bread in the mixture and grill it in a skillet with butter. Sometimes I melt brown sugar with a little water and add chopped banana or strawberry on top. I do not have fresh fruit on this day, and they've asked for honey, as both like to pour it overtop. Helena prefers jataí honey, while Maria goes with tubuna. This morning, just to tease her sister, Maria lobs a large amount of jataí honey on Helena's toast. Helena gives a little whimper of protest, and I have to calm them down.

It's early, and we are dressed for a tennis lesson. When I think about my life, I feel satisfied. We live in the house that I chose and could purchase thanks to my and my husband's efforts. We are in the city I love, where my work is respected, and where I find the best ingredients to cook with. I'm one of the few chefs in Curitiba who owns their restaurant. I don't have significant debts, and many new adventures are on my horizon.

I take my cup of hot coffee, open the sliding door, and go outside. It is heartwarming to have Snow greet me so enthusiastically. I turn right and look at my small vegetable garden, with the herbs I like to use for cooking. I always have parsley, three or four varieties of mint, rosemary, coriander, chives, and two kinds of basil. Tomatoes, cucumber, pumpkin, lettuce, spinach, carrots, and sometimes beets (beetroots) also grow there. It's hot, and the manduri and jataí native bees from the boxes at the garden entrance are agitated.

I identify with the bees, this big group of insects, the vast majority of which are female, that follow the strong and tireless queen. They spend the day looking for the best ingredients to produce wax, propolis, and honey. As bees visit plants seeking food, pollen catches on their bodies and passes between plants, fertilizing them—pollination.

I see a clear turning point in my career. Shortly after I sold the brasserie MB, I started stress-control training with Nilzo Andrade, a professional working with CEOs, athletes, chefs, and managers on a program that combines yoga, breath training, and other stress-management techniques. We recognized that while I could multi-task and juggle my passions, I needed to improve the way I managed my emotions and learn to channel my energies into the things that truly mattered to me. And I needed to hire someone to manage the cash at the restaurant. After some months of practice, I was able to transform the kitchen into a calm environment, and I learned how to prioritize what is essential. That was 2016, the year I became a mother, giving birth to Helena, and then Maria was born the following year.

Today, Manu is the size I always wanted—a fine-dining restaurant with five tables that serves a tasting menu and is open for dinner only, from Wednesday to Saturday. As a restaurant, we built in three days of rest, even before the pandemic created the trend.

I never work on Sundays. If I am in Brazil, this is the day I go to mass and play sports or cook for friends and family. Like the generations before me, I put all my heart into thinking about what to prepare, how to set the table, and what drinks I'll serve for those I love and who are always there for me.

I allocate two working days only to resolving all administrative concerns and contacting my suppliers. On Mondays and Tuesdays, I work from home, so I have more time with my daughters. From Wednesday to Saturday, I go to the restaurant. Even on more complicated days, I never return home later than 11 p.m.

As soon as she finishes her French toast, Maria opens the glass door and comes to rescue me from my daydream. It's time to start a new day. Our tennis class will begin in twenty minutes, and I will go to the restaurant in the afternoon to welcome my guests with a big smile. At the end of the night, I will say my goodbyes to each diner, thanking them for having chosen to eat my food at my restaurant.

Connection

Connection around food. I like the simplicity, history, and affection behind each product. My understanding of food changes completely when I'm in contact with the earth. Planting, tending, waiting, and harvesting become a relationship. This relationship grows as soon as I see the miracle in my hands. That is why the ingredient is my biggest inspiration.

Spinach, lard, and lemon

Classics are classics. This was one of the first snacks served at Manu. It was on the tasting menu for quite a while, because it was my favorite for a few years. But removing mental barriers is part of the creative process. We have to evolve our minds, grow, look to the horizon, and overcome the fear of not being able to create something better.

Serves 4

For the tempura batter	60 g all-purpose (plain) flour 120 ml chilled sparkling water salt, to season
For the radish mayonnaise	50 g mini radishes 120 ml whole (full-fat) milk 250 ml sunflower oil 10 ml lemon juice salt, to season
For the lemon gel	50 g sugar 45 ml water 1 gelatin sheet 38 ml lemon juice
To serve	10 g radish 200 ml sunflower oil 8 spinach leaves salt, to season 10 g lard, thinly sliced and cut into 8 (¾-inch/2-cm) squares 4 micro basil leaves

Tempura batter In a bowl, whisk together the flour and sparkling water until smooth. Season with salt and refrigerate until needed.

Radish mayonnaise Dehydrate the radishes whole at 104°F (40°C) for 4 hours. Transfer the radishes to a blender, add the milk, and blend on high speed to extract the flavor. Strain the mixture through a chinois and refrigerate for 1 hour.

Transfer the chilled radish milk to a blender and blend on high speed. With the motor still running, gradually pour in the oil in a stream, blending until emulsified. Add the lemon juice and season with salt. Pour the mayonnaise into a plastic squeeze bottle and refrigerate until needed.

Lemon gel Combine the sugar and water in a saucepan and cook over medium heat until syrupy. Remove from the heat.

Hydrate the gelatin in the lemon juice. Add the gelatin mixture to the syrup at 131°F (55°C) and stir until dissolved. Transfer to a container, then refrigerate to set. Once firm, pass the gelatin slowly through a sieve to break it up and achieve a gel-like appearance. Put in a plastic squeeze bottle and store in the refrigerator.

To serve Using a mandolin, finely slice the radish, then cut the slices into a thin julienne. Place the radish slices in a bowl of ice water for 2 minutes. Drain, then transfer to a plate lined with paper towel to drain excess water.

Heat the oil in a skillet to 338°F (170°C). Dip the spinach leaves in the tempura batter, then deep-fry the leaves, one at a time, in the hot oil for 3 minutes, or until golden. Transfer the leaves to a plate lined with paper towel to drain. Season with salt.

Place 2 warm leaves on each plate. Cover with a slice of lard. Make a circle of lemon gel around the lard. Top with julienned radish and a drop of radish mayonnaise. Finish with a micro basil leaf, placed on top of the radish mayonnaise.

Squid and young coconut

My family loves to drink coconut water. I always have liters of it at home. When we are at the beach and drink all the water from the fresh coconut there, I always ask that the coconut be cut in half, so that I can eat the flesh with a spoon. It has a unique texture that reminds me of seafood. I had that idea in mind when I created this dish.

Serves 4

For the coconut base	180 ml fresh coconut water 15 g tapioca pearls
For the squid ink salsa	100 ml olive oil 40 g red onion 1 pimenta de cheiro (green chile pepper) 1 chopped Roma tomato 40 g squid ink 50 ml Creamy Fish Stock (see page 122) 30 ml emerina native bee honey
For the squid tartare	200 g mini squid 120 g fresh young coconut meat salt, to season black pepper, to season zest of 1 lemon

Coconut base Combine the coconut water and tapioca pearls and cook in a saucepan over medium heat for 20 minutes. Strain, then refrigerate until needed.

Squid ink salsa Heat the olive oil in a skillet over medium heat. Add the onion and sauté for about 15 minutes, until golden. Add the chile and tomato and bring to a boil. Add the squid ink and fish stock, boil for 10 minutes, then pass through a sieve. Stir in the honey. Refrigerate until needed.

Squid tartare Separate the squid's head from the body. Blanch in hot water for 40 seconds, then transfer to a bowl of ice water. Cut into ½-inch (1-cm) cubes. Cut the coconut into ½-inch (1-cm) cubes. Combine the coconut and squid in a bowl. Season with salt, pepper, and lemon zest, mixing well.

To serve Place some squid tartare in the center of each plate. Spoon the coconut base around it and finish with a few drops of squid ink salsa.

Scallops, yogurt, and dill

This is such a simple and delicate recipe—and captures the perfect cook point for scallops. The scallops go well with the yogurt seasoned with scallop eggs, and with the touch of dill.

Serves 4

For the dill oil	170 g dill
	120 ml grapeseed oil
For the yogurt	400 g fresh grated coconut
	200 g plain (natural) yogurt
	150 ml tucupi
	4 scallop coral
	1 makrut lime leaf
	½ stalk lemongrass
For the crispy black rice	250 g wild rice
	sunflower oil, for deep-frying
	salt and black pepper, to season
For the scallops	8 high-quality live scallops
	10 ml olive oil
To serve	chopped dill, for garnish

Dill oil

Place 120 g of dill and the grapeseed oil in a Thermomix and mix for 6 minutes. Char the remaining 50 g of dill over coals or using a kitchen torch. Add the charred dill to the Thermomix and mix for 1 minute. Then strain.

Yogurt

Combine all the ingredients in a blender and blend well. Strain.

Crispy black rice

Heat the oil in a skillet until it reaches 450°F to 480°F (230°C to 250°C). Working in batches, place a shallow layer of wild rice in a sieve and lower it into the hot oil. Deep-fry the rice until they burst open. (This happens almost immediately.) Transfer the popped rice to a plate lined with paper towel. Season with salt and pepper. Repeat with the remaining wild rice.

Scallops

Clean the scallops and set them aside. Before serving, brush one side of the scallops with a little olive oil, then pass a kitchen torch over that side of the scallop only.

To serve

Spread the yogurt on each plate and arrange the scallops on top. Finish with the dill oil and garnish with chopped dill.

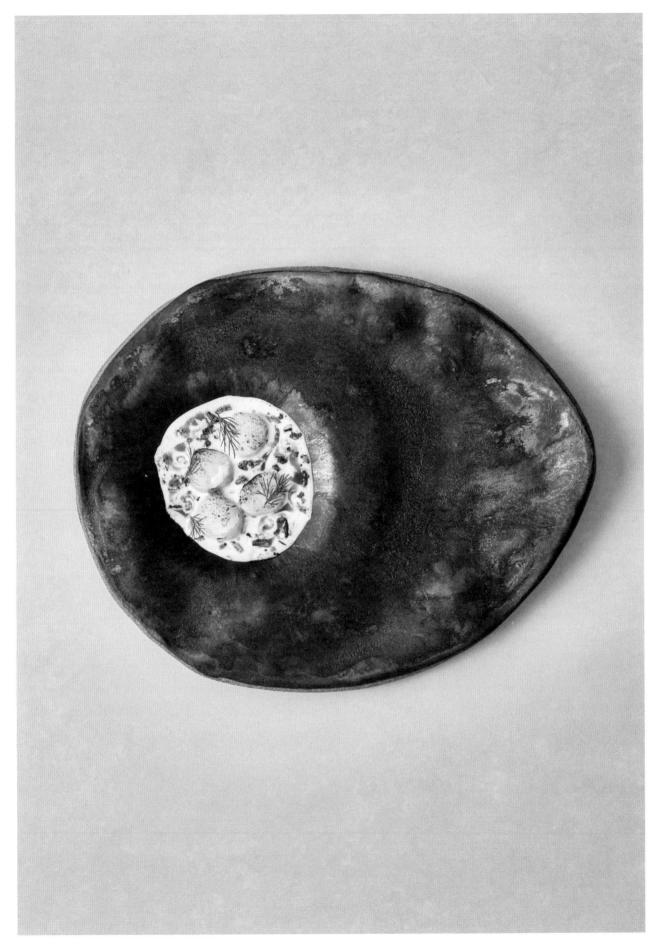

Oyster, strawberry, and lime snow

Cooking means respecting the timing of things: respecting the product and deciding its best "outfit." Our native oysters are among the best in the world, briny like the sea where they are found. Serving them with strawberry and lime snow is magical.

Serves 4

For the strawberry	50 g strawberries (about 2) 0.5 g fleur de sel
For the lime snow	60 g plain (natural) yogurt 30 ml heavy (double) cream 25 ml lime juice zest of 1 lime salt, to season
For the coconut sauce	50 ml Coconut Milk (see page 68) 10 ml rice vinegar zest of 1 lemon
For the oyster	4 fresh oysters
To serve	fleur de sel, to season 4 cilantro (coriander) leaves

Strawberry   Remove the green leafy top from the strawberries. Place the strawberries and fleur de sel in a vacuum bag. Seal the bag under a full vacuum and leave it closed for 24 hours. After 24 hours, remove the strawberries. Cut into brunoise and set aside.

Lime snow   In a bowl, mix together all the ingredients. Place the mixture in a freezer-proof container and freeze for 24 hours. Remove from the freezer and scrape with a fork. Store the shaved lime snow in the freezer until needed.

Coconut sauce   In a bowl, blend all the ingredients together using an immersion blender. Set aside.

Oyster   Preheat a skillet over high heat. Open the oyster shells and put the oyster meat in the skillet. Sear for 5 seconds, then transfer to snack plates.

To serve   Season the oysters with the fleur de sel. Arrange some strawberries on top, drizzle with the coconut sauce, and top with a small cilantro (coriander) leaf. Cover half of each oyster with a spoonful of lime snow and serve immediately.

Tucupi, caper,
and pork tartare

Be proud of your roots, be proud of your land, be proud of your family and culture. They are my greatest inspiration. The Moura pork we use represents my land and my state (page III).

Serves 4

For the pork tartare	1 g salt
	1 g sugar
	250 g pork tenderloin

| For the tucupi emulsion | 80 g brown butter (beurre noisette) |
| | 100 ml tucupi |

| For the crispy capers | 50 g canned capers, drained |
| | 10 ml olive oil |

To serve	salt, to season
	black pepper, to season
	olive oil, to season
	2 g coffee beans
	4 green oxalis sprouts (optional)

Pork tartare Combine the salt and sugar in a small bowl. Rub the mixture over the tenderloin, then place the meat on a wire rack set over a rimmed baking sheet. Cure in the refrigerator for 4 hours. Pat dry with paper towel and cut into ¼-inch (5-mm) cubes.

Tucupi emulsion In a small skillet, bring the brown butter (beurre noisette) and tucupi to a slight boil and cook until emulsified. Keep at 104°F (40°C).

Crispy capers Pat dry the capers with paper towel. Place them in a nonstick skillet and warm over medium heat until they start to release salt onto the bottom of the pan. Add the olive oil and fry until the capers open.

Transfer the capers to a plate lined with paper towel to drain. Put the capers in a dehydrator for 30 minutes. Chop them, then set aside.

To serve Place the pork in a bowl and season with salt, pepper, olive oil, and chopped capers. Place some of this tartare in the center of each plate. Spoon the tucupi emulsion overtop to cover. Use a microplane to grate some coffee bean onto each plate, then garnish each plate with an oxalis sprout, if using.

Mussels, endive, and lard

I fight for food quality, diversity, and the small producers in my home state of Paraná. Our crustaceans come from small producers in southern Brazil. I love the combination of vegetables and orange juice—it reminds me of the salads I prepare at home. At the restaurant, I love to match the two with the fantastic seafood I receive every week.

Serves 4

For the mussel sauce	
	150 g chopped onion
	50 g brown butter (beurre noisette)
	3 g grated garlic
	120 g chopped fennel
	600 g cooked mussel meat
	200 ml white wine
	400 ml Coconut Milk (see page 68)
	400 ml whole (full-fat) milk
	200 ml heavy (double) cream

For the citrus caramel	
	2 oranges
	2 mandarin oranges
	1 grapefruit
	1 lemon
	1 lime
	1 rangpur lime

For the endives	
	4 endives
	100 g brown butter (beurre noisette)
	400 ml orange juice
	50 ml Citrus Caramel (see above)
	50 g cubed cold butter

To serve	
	20 g Boursin cheese
	8 slices lard

Mussel sauce Braise the onion in the brown butter (beurre noisette) in a skillet over medium heat. Add the garlic and stir to mix well. Add the fennel and sauté for 15 minutes, or until the vegetables are caramelized. Add the mussels and cook until all the liquid has evaporated. Pour in the white wine and cook for 5 minutes, or until most of the liquid has evaporated.

Pour in the coconut milk and milk and bring to a boil. Boil for 20 minutes. Transfer to a blender, add the cream, and blend for 10 minutes on high speed. Strain.

Citrus caramel Juice all the citruses. Combine the juices in a saucepan and heat over medium-high heat for about 15 minutes, until reduced by half.

Endives Cut the endives in half lengthwise. Place cut side down in a skillet with the brown butter (beurre noisette). Cook for 3 minutes, or until the center is tender. Turn over, add the orange juice, and simmer until the juice is reduced by a quarter. Pour in the citrus caramel and add the butter cubes little by little, scraping the bottom of the pan with a spoon to deglaze.

To serve Warm the mussel sauce. Spoon some mussel sauce onto each plate and crumble over some cheese. Top with 2 pieces of endive and then 2 slices of lard, spooning the endive sauce overtop. Serve immediately.

Cauliflower, passion fruit, and peanuts

Cauliflower is beautiful and delicate, like a flower, yet can have a strong taste or no taste at all, depending on the way it's prepared. I delight in its flexibility and in how well it combines with all kinds of ingredients and textures.

Our cauliflower and bottarga dish (page III) became well known, and diners have also really enjoyed our cauliflower and cashew milk dish. I love the sourness of the passion fruit combined with the umami from the way we cook the cauliflower and the unusual addition of peanuts, rarely used by chefs but which is one of the most incredible indigenous Brazilian ingredients.

Serves 4

For the cauliflower	50 g butter
	400 g cauliflower
	300 ml water

For the passion fruit fried milk Part 1	300 g butter
	150 g cauliflower florets
	200 ml whole (full-fat) milk
	110 g passion fruit juice and seeds

Part 2	100 g brown butter (beurre noisette)
	120 ml whole (full-fat) milk
	50 ml heavy (double) cream

For the peanut foam	300 g peanuts
	350 ml whole (full-fat) milk
	200 ml heavy (double) cream
	50 ml rice vinegar
	pinch of salt

To serve	20 ml olive oil
	2 g sage
	fleur de sel, for sprinkling
	5 g bottarga

Cauliflower Choose a large enough saucepan to fit the whole cauliflower. Heat the butter in the pan over high heat. Add the whole cauliflower and fry on each side. Pour in 150 ml of water. Cover and cook for 10–15 minutes, until very soft but not falling apart. If all the water evaporates, add the remaining 150 ml. Remove the cauliflower from the pan and set it aside to cool. Cut into florets. Reserve the cooking liquid.

Passion fruit fried milk Part 1 Heat the butter in a skillet over low heat. Add the cauliflower florets and cook over low heat for 1 hour.

Drain, reserving the butter. In a large saucepan, bring 185 g of the cauliflower butter to a boil. Pour in the milk (this will cause a reaction, so it's important that the pan is large) and boil for about 20 minutes. (In Brazil, we call this process "frying the milk.") Turn off the heat and let the milk sit for 2 minutes, then add the passion fruit juice and seeds. Using an immersion blender, blend for 5 minutes. Set aside to cool.

Part 2 Bring the brown butter (beurre noisette) to a boil in a large saucepan. Add the milk and cream and "fry" (as in part 1) by allowing the mixture to boil for 15 minutes, then reducing the heat to low and cook for another 3 minutes. Turn off the heat and let the mixture sit for 1 minute. Using an immersion blender, blend until smooth. Add the passion fruit mixture from part 1 and blend at high speed for 2 minutes, or until homogenized and creamy.

Peanut foam Preheat the oven to 350°F (180°C).

Spread the peanuts on a baking sheet and lightly toast in the oven for 10 minutes. Transfer the peanuts to a blender and blend with the milk until you have a homogeneous paste. Pass through a sieve.

Transfer the mixture to a saucepan and gently simmer. Stir in the cream. Remove from the heat and add the vinegar and salt. While still warm, transfer to a blender and blend to mix well. Pass through the sieve again.

Put the mixture in a siphon bottle with 2 charges. Put it in the refrigerator for at least 4 hours. Dispense the foam into a squeeze bottle.

To serve Heat the oil in a skillet over medium heat. Add the sage and fry for 2 minutes. Set aside.

Pour the reserved cauliflower cooking liquid into a saucepan, add the cauliflower, and cook over high heat for 5 minutes. You want the cauliflower florets to remain whole.

Pour some passion fruit milk into each bowl, then add a few cauliflower florets and cover with the cauliflower liquid. Put some peanut foam next to the cauliflower and finish with a pinch of fleur de sel. Serve with tiny slices of bottarga and the fried sage.

Grouper, peach palm, and bone marrow

Peach palm, native to tropical forests and found throughout Amazonia, is usually cultivated by smallholders in the agroforestry system. This long-living plant can live for more than sixty years. It has a perfect texture and a subtle and persistent flavor that goes well with the grouper from South Brazil.

Serves 4

For the peach palm **Part 1**	350 g peach palm
	400 ml water
	50 ml rice vinegar
	15 g butter
	salt, to season
Part 2	100 g butter
	20 ml sunflower oil
	200 g chopped onion
	45 g garlic
	1 roasted pimenta de cheiro (green chile pepper)
	bunch of cilantro (coriander)
	5 sprigs mint
	5 sprigs thyme
	5 sprigs oregano
	2 stalks lemongrass
	2 kg fresh tuna
	150 g grated ginger
	120 ml light soy sauce
	120 ml black tucupi
	80 g sugar
	2 pink lemons, peeled and cut into 4 pieces
	3 L water
For the marrow	2 beef marrow bones, cut in half and into 6-inch (15-cm) lengths
	small bunch of cilantro (coriander)
	small sprig of mint
For the grouper	50 ml olive oil, plus extra for brushing
	4 grouper fillets, with skin

Peach palm Part 1   Juice the peach palm in a juicer. Place both the juice and pulp in a saucepan, add the water, and cook over medium heat until reduced by half. Add the vinegar, butter, and salt. Cook over low heat for 2 hours. Strain the mixture through a chinois and set aside.

Part 2   Melt the butter and oil in a skillet over high heat. Add the onion, garlic, and chile. Reduce the heat to medium. Add the cilantro (coriander), mint, thyme, oregano, and lemongrass and increase the heat to high. Boil for 1 minute, then add the tuna and ginger, stirring carefully until the tuna has browned. Add the soy sauce and tucupi and bring to another boil. Add the sugar and stir well to caramelize. Add the lemons and water. Cook for 55 minutes. Remove the pan from the heat, cover, and set aside for 1 hour at room temperature. Strain, then return to medium heat and cook for 2 hours, or until reduced by 40%.

Marrow   Preheat the oven to 350°F (180°C).

Place the marrow bones in a roasting pan and bake for 20 minutes. Remove from the oven, remove the marrow from the bone, and add it to a blender along with the herbs. Strain through a chinois and return to the pan. Keep warm.

Grouper   Preheat a combination oven to 350°F (180°C) with 100% humidity.

Heat the oil in a skillet over high heat. Fry the fish, skin side down, in the oil, then transfer to a baking sheet and brush the top with olive oil. Bake for 1 minute and 30 seconds. Before serving, pass a kitchen torch over the fish.

To serve   Mix half of the peach palm mixture from part 1 with one-third of the mixture from part 2. (Save the rest for another day.) Place 2 spoonfuls of the mixture on the plates, then arrange some grouper in the center. Finish with the marrow.

Yellowtail, fennel, and marrow

The Manu tasting menu always includes a fresh fish dish. I receive such high-quality fish every day that it is impossible not to prepare them. The recipes change according to the fish I receive. I love the yellowtail found in the cold waters of South Brazil. It is commonly used for sushi. The cook point is key to this dish: the fish has to be quickly grilled (griddled), just before going to the table. Be careful not to overcook the fillet. I love the sweetness of the fennel sauce mixed with the light acidity of the coconut foam and the comfort that comes from the marrow beef sauce.

Serves 4

For the yellowtail	5 g sugar
	3 g salt
	2 g sea lettuce, dehydrated and ground
	300 g skinless yellowtail, cleaned
For the fennel sauce	300 g fennel bulb
	100 g cashew nuts
	350 ml whole (full-fat) milk
	50 g dill
	100 ml Creamy Fish Stock (see page 122)
	1 lime
	50 g cold butter
	salt, to season
For the marrow	80 g beef marrow
	2 g chopped white (button) mushrooms
	30 g brown butter (beurre noisette)
	zest of ½ lime
For the coconut foam	80 ml Coconut Milk (see page 68)
	20 g plain (natural) yogurt
	zest of 1 lime
To serve	olive oil, for frying
	fennel fronds, for garnish

Yellowtail Combine the sugar, salt, and sea lettuce powder in a small bowl. Sprinkle over both sides of the yellowtail. Place on a wire rack set over a baking sheet and place in the refrigerator for 1 hour to cure. Pat dry with paper towel.

Fennel sauce Preheat the oven to 329°F (165°C).

Wrap the fennel in aluminum foil and bake for 1 hour, flipping after 30 minutes.

Blend the cashews and milk in a blender until smooth. Add the hot fennel and dill and blend on high speed for 5 minutes. Strain the mixture through a chinois into a saucepan. Add the fish stock and warm over medium heat.

Heat a heavy-bottomed skillet over medium heat. Cut the lime in half and toast the halves in the hot skillet until caramelized. Squeeze the caramelized lime over the fennel sauce. Add the butter and, using an immersion blender, blend the sauce until emulsified. Season with salt.

Marrow Melt the marrow in a heavy-bottomed skillet over low heat. Pass through a sieve to remove the excess fat. Using an immersion blender, blend until smooth and strain again. Add the chopped mushrooms, brown butter (beurre noisette), and lime zest.

Coconut foam Heat the coconut milk and yogurt in a small saucepan over medium heat. Blend with an immersion blender until foamy. Add the lime zest.

To serve Heat a nonstick skillet. Use a drizzle of olive oil to fry the fish for about 2 minutes on each side. Meanwhile, heat the fennel sauce, then use an immersion blender to create a foam. Put 100 ml of fennel sauce in a deep dish. Cut the yellowtail into 4 equal pieces. Place on the fennel sauce. Drizzle with a spoonful of marrow sauce, then add some coconut foam. Garnish with fennel fronds. Serve immediately.

Seaweed, mushroom, and dill

This dish came about when I discovered I could forage mushrooms and seaweed in Santa Catarina and Paraná respectively. I would spend hours in the countryside and at the beach looking for them. I would return from my adventures with loads of them. So I created powders and sauces that were mushroom- and seaweed-based for recipes such as this.

Serves 4

For the granola	200 g medium oats
	100 g brown sugar
	14 g flaxseed
	50 g chopped cashew nuts
	30 g raisins
	30 g raw sunflower seeds
	20 g flaked coconut
	8 g salt
	25 ml Coconut Milk (see page 68)
	15 ml honey
	8 ml vanilla extract
For the dill oil	200 g dill
	200 ml grapeseed oil
For the seaweed sauce	20 g toasted nori sheets
	150 ml cold water
	70 ml light soy sauce
	25 ml lemon juice
	2 g xanthan gum
For the mushroom powder	400 g shimeji mushrooms, dehydrated at 150°F (65°C) for 4 hours
	200 g shiitake mushrooms, dehydrated at 150°F (65°C) for 4 hours
To serve	200 g fior di latte gelato

Granola   Preheat the oven to 350°F (180°C).

In a food processor, combine the oats, brown sugar, and flaxseed and process on high speed to a fine flour. Transfer the mixture to a bowl. Add the remaining ingredients and mix well.

Spread on a baking sheet and bake for 20 minutes, or until crunchy. Set aside to cool.

Dill oil   Put the dill and grapeseed oil in a Thermomix and mix at high speed at 150°F (65°C) for 10 minutes. Strain through a cheesecloth (muslin) into a bowl and let rest for 12 hours at 39°F (4°C). Separate the oil from the dill water. Refrigerate the dill oil until needed. Discard the dill water.

Seaweed sauce   Put all the ingredients in a Thermomix and mix at high speed for 5 minutes.

Mushroom powder   Process the dehydrated mushrooms in a blender or food processor at high speed until a fine powder forms. Sift, then store in an airtight container.

To serve   Put 1 teaspoon of seaweed sauce into each bowl. Scatter a little bit of granola over the sauce, then drizzle the dill oil around the seaweed sauce. Place a quenelle of gelato on top of the granola. Sprinkle mushroom powder over the gelato. Serve immediately.

Apple and tonka bean

I love apples: the acidity, crunchiness, and sweetness. In this recipe, we use two types of apples—Fuji, which has a lot of water and is very sweet, and the green apple, which is tarter. We balance them with tonka bean, or cumaru, a tropical seed from the Amazon known for its vanilla scent. This is a classic dish with a Brazilian touch.

Serves 4

For the apple cream	400 g Fuji apple
	1 lemon
	70 g sugar

For the ice cream	1 tonka bean (cumaru)
	330 ml whole (full-fat) milk
	120 g sugar
	90 g sour cream
	100 g egg yolks

For the apple petals	75 ml water
	75 ml apple cider vinegar
	75 g sugar
	1 Fuji apple

For the apple crumble	75 g room-temperature butter
	75 g sugar
	75 g all-purpose (plain) flour
	130 g grated unpeeled green apple

| To serve | micro basil, for garnish |

Apple cream Cut the unpeeled apples into medium cubes. Squeeze the lemon juice over the chopped apple.

In a skillet, heat the sugar over medium-low heat until dissolved and caramelized (it shouldn't be too dark). Add the apples, cover, and cook for 9 minutes, or until very tender.

Transfer the apples to a blender and blend until smooth. Set aside.

Ice cream Grate the tonka bean into a saucepan. Add the milk, sugar, sour cream, and egg yolks. Heat to 180°F (82°C), stirring until thickened. Pour the mixture into a pacotizing beaker. Seal the pacotizing beaker, then freeze at −8°F (−22°C) for at least 24 hours.

Apple petals Combine the water, vinegar, and sugar in a saucepan and bring to a boil. Boil for 20 minutes, or until the vinegar odor is gone and the syrup is thick. Let cool. Using a mandolin, thinly slice the apple. Place the slices in the syrup, so they become malleable enough to assemble the "petals." Assemble the apple petals by layering the apple slices upright in a 1½-inch (4-cm) deep ring mold with a 1¼-inch (3-cm) circumference. Refrigerate until needed.

Apple crumble Preheat the oven to 300°F (150°C).

In a large bowl, combine the butter, sugar, flour, and grated green apple, mixing well. Spread on a baking sheet and bake for 10 minutes. Stir the crumble, then bake for another 10 minutes. Set aside.

To serve Fill the apple petal ring with the apple cream, then gently remove the mold. Place on the plate, top with the apple crumble, and finish with a quenelle of tonka bean ice cream and micro basil.

Fermented corn
and red berries

Sometimes, Brazilian food journalists call me the queen of acidity. They have a point; I do like it. The sweet desserts served at the restaurant must have a sour twist. In this recipe, the fermented flour adds that element to the dough, and the red berries do the same for the filling. Besides all that, the color combination in this recipe is incredibly simple and beautiful.

Serves 4

For the fermented corn flour	500 g corn cobs
For the berry filling	75 g raspberries 75 g strawberries 125 g chopped white chocolate 35 ml heavy (double) cream
For the macaron	62.5 g Fermented Corn Flour (see above) 30 g all-purpose (plain) flour 55 g sugar 55 g egg whites 55 g confectioners' (icing) sugar
To serve	edible flowers, to decorate

Fermented corn flour Cut off the corn kernels very close to the cob. Put them in a vacuum bag and seal, removing as much air as possible. Let cool in the refrigerator for 5–7 days, until the bag swells. Mash the kernels coarsely and put on a Silpat. Let them dry out in the oven at 95°F (35°C) for 14 hours. Process the dried kernels to a fine flour, then pass through a fine sieve.

Berry filling Preheat the oven to 140°F (60°C).

Spread the berries on a Silpat and bake until dehydrated, about 9 hours. Remove from the oven and let cool, then transfer to a blender and blend to a powder. In a bain-marie, heat the white chocolate and cream, stirring to mix well. Add the berry powder and mix well. Chill in the refrigerator.

Macaron Blend the fermented corn flour and flour, then pass through an ultra-fine sieve. Reserve.

In a bain-marie, mix together the sugar and egg whites until smooth. Do not let the mixture go above 140°F (60°C). Beat the mixture on maximum speed, adding the confectioners' (icing) sugar little by little, until doubled in size. Use a rubber spatula to add the flours to the mixture, gently stirring until homogenous.

Pour the mixture into a pastry (piping) bag fitted with a round tip. Make macarons 1½ inches (4 cm) in diameter on a Silpat. Let rest for 25 minutes, or until a skin forms. Preheat the oven to 293°F (145°C), then bake the macarons for 15 minutes.

To serve Pipe the berry filling into the macarons. Decorate with flower petals.

Priprioca and passion fruit skin 1.0

Priprioca is an Amazonian root that is often used in perfumes, but it can also be cooked. The Indigenous people use this incredible root as a unique seasoning—it has a distinct flavor and smell.

Serves 4

For the priprioca dulce de leche	500 ml whole (full-fat) milk
	125 g sugar
	8 ml corn syrup
	5 g grated priprioca root
	0.5 g baking soda (bicarbonate of soda)
	0.5 g salt
For the passion fruit crisp	150 g fresh passion fruit pulp
	50 ml water
	35 g tapioca pearls
To serve	100 g Yogurt Ice Cream (see page 78)

Priprioca dulce de leche — Combine all the ingredients in a heavy-bottomed saucepan and bring to a boil over low heat. Boil for about 4 hours, stirring frequently, until creamy and a light caramel color. Remove from the heat and let cool. Transfer to a container and refrigerate until needed.

Passion fruit crisp — In a small saucepan, combine the passion fruit pulp and water and bring to a boil. Reduce the heat to medium and cook for 10 minutes. Strain through a chinois, discarding the seeds.

Return the liquid to the saucepan, add the tapioca pearls, and cook over medium heat for 10 minutes, stirring constantly with a whisk. Strain again, then pass the liquid through a chinois and refrigerate until cool. Using a rubber spatula, spread the mixture on a Silpat and dehydrate for about 12 hours at 100°F (38°C), until crispy and glossy.

To serve — Put a spoonful of the priprioca dulce de leche on each plate. Top with a quenelle of yogurt ice cream and scatter irregular pieces of passion fruit crisp overtop.

Petit Fours

In 2017, I created a range of petit fours to accompany the new coffee service at Manu. As I wanted to honor my beloved grandmother Guegué, we made the cantucci (biscotti) in the same manner as our Italian ancestors. I also developed an oat cookie that reminds me of the ones we had in Maringá. It was such a joyful experience to brainstorm desserts that pastry chef Vanessa and I decided to serve these variations with coffee to our guests.

(Clockwise from top left) Cheese cookies, oat cookies (page 217), guava cookies (page 221), tonka bean brigadeiro (page 218), cartucci (page 219), beijinho and puxuri (page 220), and chococo.

Oat cookies

In 2016, I received a visit from a master coffee roaster who said my coffee service could improve (page 106). When we began to serve specialty coffees at Manu, I made various petit fours to go along with them. I remembered the oat cookies I used to eat as a child, and Vanessa and I developed this recipe. My daughters, Maria and Helena, love these cookies, and sometimes I ask Vanessa to bake a few extra, for me to take them some.

Serves 4

For the cookies
55 g rolled oats
55 g rye flour
45 g butter
20 g brown sugar
2.5 g baking soda
(bicarbonate of soda)
pinch of ground cinnamon
20 g egg

In a food processor, combine the oats, rye flour, and butter on maximum speed. Transfer the mixture to a bowl, add the brown sugar, baking soda (bicarbonate of soda), cinnamon, and egg and knead well. Wrap the dough in plastic wrap (clingfilm) and refrigerate for 1–2 hours.

Preheat the oven to 311°F (155°C). Place the dough between 2 sheets of parchment paper and roll out to a thickness of ¼ inch (5 mm). Cut out 1–inch (2.5-cm) circles and bake on a Silpat for 15 minutes, or until golden. Remove from the oven and let cool before serving.

Tonka bean brigadeiro

A constant presence at children's party tables, *brigadeiro*, a kind of chocolate truffle, is a tradition in Brazil. Some people say it isn't a party without them. Those outside Brazil tend to think it is too sweet, and I agree with them. So this recipe is my version of brigadeiro, with delicious Amazonian dark chocolate and tonka bean (cumaru) to accentuate the bitterness.

Serves 4

For the **brigadeiro**	1 L whole (full-fat) milk
	150 g sugar
	120 g unsweetened cocoa powder (63% cocoa)
	30 g butter
	7 g hydrated tapioca flour
	14 ml water
	1 tonka bean (cumaru)

In a large saucepan, combine the milk, sugar, cocoa powder, and butter. Bring to a boil over high heat, without stirring, and boil until reduced by a fifth. Reduce the heat to medium.

In a small bowl, dissolve the tapioca flour in the water. Add to the pan, gently stirring to prevent it from sticking to the bottom of the pan. Grate the tonka bean (cumaru) into the pan and stir to combine.

Transfer the mixture to a bowl and chill in the refrigerator for 1 hour before serving. Roll the dough into hazelnut-sized balls and serve immediately.

Cantucci

This recipe is a small tribute to Italy, where I learned so much. Italians usually have some cantucci (biscotti) on hand whenever coffee is served. When we upped the quality of our coffee at the restaurant, I decided to serve it with cantucci. Here, I've adapted a family heirloom recipe.

Serves 4

For the cantucci
200 g almonds
500 g all-purpose (plain) flour
350 g sugar
4 eggs
15 ml honey
15 g baking powder
5 g salt

Preheat the oven to 350°F (180°C). Grease a baking sheet.

Bring a small saucepan of water to a boil, then add the almonds and boil for 5 minutes. Drain, then remove the skins. Spread on an ungreased baking sheet and bake for 15 minutes, or until dried out. Reduce the oven temperature to 300°F (150°C). Reserving a small handful, transfer the almonds to a food processor or blender and blend into medium pieces.

In a bowl, combine the flour, sugar, eggs, honey, baking powder, and salt. Add all the almonds and mix well. Roll the dough into logs about 4–6 inches (10–15 cm) long and about 1 inch (2.5 cm) in diameter, and bake on a greased baking sheet for 10 minutes. Remove from the oven, keeping the oven on, and let cool to room temperature, about 15 minutes. Cut the logs on the diagonal into ½-inch (1-cm) slices. Return to the oven and bake for another 7–9 minutes, until golden.

Beijinho and puxuri

Beijinho de coco, or "coconut kiss," is another sweet that we often have at children's parties in Brazil. It is nearly the same as our *brigadeiro* recipe (page 218), but with coconut instead of cocoa powder. Our version has grated puxuri, a seed from Amazonia that has a delicious aroma. We also use a very good fresh grated coconut.

Serves 4

For the beijinho	320 ml condensed milk
	70 g butter
	150 g fresh grated coconut
	2 g grated puxuri
	10 g butter, for greasing
	50 g powdered milk

Combine the condensed milk, butter, and coconut in a saucepan. Bring to a boil and stir continuously for 15 minutes until the mixture lifts off the bottom of the pan. Remove from the heat and add the puxuri. Transfer to a glass bowl and let cool, then sit at room temperature for 4 hours. With greased hands, shape the mixture into hazelnut-sized balls. Dust with the powdered milk.

Guava cookies

Goiabinha, cookies filled with guava paste, are common in Brazilian student lunch boxes. The guava tree is common in Brazil, even in big cities. Many people make wonderful guava paste with the red fruit and sugar, a popular dessert on its own, though some like to eat it with cheese. I have a good supplier of guava paste and was happy to develop this recipe to cap the menu at Manu.

Serves 4

For the cookies
40 g room-temperature butter
135 g eggs
15 g sugar
4 g baking powder
2 g salt
200 g all-purpose (plain) flour
300 g guava paste

Preheat the oven to 300°F (150°C).

In a bowl, combine the butter, eggs, sugar, baking powder, and salt. Add the flour little by little and mix until a smooth dough forms. Let rest for 2 hours in the refrigerator.

Place the dough between 2 Silpats. Using a rolling pin, roll out the dough to a thickness of ¼ inch (5 mm). Cut the guava paste into 1½-inch (3-cm) strips. Using a 2¾-inch (7-cm) cookie cutter, cut out circles from the dough. Gather the leftover dough and repeat until all the dough is used. Arrange a strip of guava in the center of each disk and cover it by folding the sides. Press lightly to seal.

Place the guava cookies on a Silpat and bake for 20 minutes. Let cool before serving.

Sweet popcorn

When I was a child and lived in Maringá, Claudete used to cook for our family. She often prepared some sweet popcorn for my brother and me in the afternoon. Today for me, the flavor makes me nostalgic for my childhood. I've developed this recipe with my pastry chef, Vanessa Lima, and I love that she uses coconut oil to make the caramel. It goes well with the popcorn.

Serves 4

For the popcorn	5 ml sunflower oil
	80 g popcorn kernels
For the caramel	160 g sugar
	80 ml water
	15 ml melted pequi oil or coconut oil
	1 g baking soda (bicarbonate of soda)

Popcorn — In a skillet, heat the popcorn kernels in the oil until they start to pop. Once popped, transfer the popcorn to a large bowl.

Caramel syrup — Heat the sugar and water in a small saucepan over high heat until it begins to boil. Reduce the temperature slightly to 293°F (145°C) and continue cooking until it is the color of caramel. Add the melted pequi or coconut oil and baking soda (bicarbonate of soda) and whisk.

Pour the caramel over the popcorn and, using 2 large spoons, toss to coat. Before the caramel hardens, spread the popcorn on a Silpat to cool before serving.

Index

Index

Recipe Notes

Butter is always unsalted, unless other-wise specified.

All sugar is granulated, unless otherwise specified.

All herbs are fresh, unless otherwise specified.

All cream is 36–40% fat heavy whipping cream, unless otherwise specified.

All milk is whole at 3% fat, homogenized and lightly pasteurized, unless otherwise specified.

All salt is fine sea salt, unless otherwise specified.

Cooking times are for guidance only, as individual ovens vary. If using a fan (convection) oven, follow the manufacturer's directions concerning oven temperatures. Exercise a high level of caution when following recipes involving any potentially hazardous activity, including the use of high temperatures, open flames, slaked lime, and when deep-frying. In particular, when deep-frying, add food carefully to avoid splashing, wear long sleeves, and never leave the pan unattended.

Some recipes include raw or very lightly cooked eggs, meat, or fish, and fermented products. These should be avoided by the elderly, infants, pregnant people, convalescents, and anyone with an impaired immune system.

Exercise caution when making fermented products, ensuring all equipment is spotlessly clean, and seek expert advice if in any doubt.

Exercise caution when foraging for ingredients; any foraged ingredients should be eaten only if an expert has deemed them safe to eat, and should be cleaned well before use.

As some species of mushrooms have been known to cause allergic reaction and illness, do take extra care when cooking and eating mushrooms and do seek immediate medical help if you experience a reaction after preparing or eating them.

When no quantity is specified, for example of oils, salts, and herbs used for finishing dishes or for deep-frying, quantities are discretionary and flexible.

All herbs, shoots, flowers, and leaves should be picked fresh from a clean source.

Purple oxalis sprouts are toxic in large quantities and should be used only in the specified amounts.

All spoon and cup measurements are level, unless otherwise stated.

Australian standard tablespoons are 20 ml, so Australian readers are advised to use 3 teaspoons in place of 1 tablespoon when measuring small quantities.

The oyster harvesters at Paraiso das Ostras work together with researchers to create the perfect environment for oyster cultivation.

About the Author

Manoella Buffara Ramos, known as Manu, is a Brazilian chef based in Curitiba, in southern Brazil. Since the opening of her restaurant Manu, in January 2011, she has been involved in sustainability actions, working alongside local communities to preserve the environment and Brazilian ingredients and culture. Devoted to hyperlocal and sustainable ingredients, her kitchen smells like the sea, small farms, and the Atlantic Forest. In 2022, she was awarded "Latin America's Best Female Chef" by Latin America's 50 Best Restaurants, and she continues to place on best restaurant and chef awards lists. She has traveled the world to participate in food conferences, charities, and collaborative dinners. Her next ventures include a pop-up kitchen at the Soneva hotel in the Maldives and her new restaurant Ella in New York City. Buffara lives with her husband, Dario, and two daughters, Helena and Maria, in Curitiba.

Acknowledgments

I would not have been able to write this book without the incredible support of Juliana de Oliveira (project management), Carolina Chagas (text), Lucas Correia (recipes), Jimena Agois and Helena Peixoto (photographs), Emily Takoudes (my editor), Michelle Meade (project editor) and the entire Phaidon team.

I would also like to thank Debora Teixeira, Vanessa Lima, Juli Rodrigues, Deisire Nagorski, Henrique Lorkievicz, Deibd Rodrigues, Jean Santana, Bruno Cabral, Carlos Eduardo Chaves, and Nivaldo dos Santos.

Above all, thank you to my family: my husband, children, parents, and grandparents. Your loving support, guidance, and inspiration have led me to become the person I am today.

We use the bacuri from Nininho's house to prepare the fermented welcome drinks.

The sheep at Fazenda Ferrador.

Phaidon Press Limited
2 Cooperage Yard
London
E15 2QR

Phaidon Press Inc.
65 Bleecker Street
New York, NY 10012
phaidon.com

First published 2023
© 2023 Phaidon Press Limited

ISBN:
978 1 83866 629 3 (trade edition)
978 1 83866 685 9 (signed edition)

Commissioning Editor: Emily Takoudes
Project Editor: Michelle Meade
Production Controllers: Nerissa Vales, Zuzana Cimalova, and Andie Trainer
Design: Hans Stofregen
Layouts: Cantina
Photography: All images by Jimena Agois, except for those on pages 20,
22—5, 31, 36, 88, 93—4, 175, and 178 by Helena Peixoto
Cover photograph: Radu F D/Shutterstock.com

Printed in China

The Publisher would like to thank James Brown, Carolina Chagas, Iva Cheung,
João Mota, Juliana de Oliveira, Elizabeth Parsons, Judy Phillips, Ellie Smith,
Tracey Smith, and Ana Teodoro for their contributions to the book.